Income Tax Guide for Rideshare and Contract Delivery Drivers

How to Prepare Your Tax Return When You Have Uber, Lyft, DoorDash or other Contract Driving Income

John C. White, JD

3rd Millennium Tax, LLC

Please – Help Me Make This the Best Guide Possible!

I'd love to hear from you about your experience with this guide, and with the IRS in the event that you should be audited for your rideshare income or deductions. I've tried to make this guide as complete as possible, based on my knowledge of both the tax law and the workings of the IRS, but I have no doubt that it can be improved. If you should see something I've missed, or have any suggestion for improvement, I'd like to hear from you. Hopefully, the next edition of this book can be even better. Please provide any comments at www.3rdmillenniumtax.com.

I'll also publish answers to FAQs, as they arise, at www.3rdmillenniumtax.com.

Dedication

This book is dedicated to my amazing wife Melissa, without whom none of this would be possible.

Table of Contents

5

INTRODUCTION

The Complexity of the Internal Revenue Code

You may have heard your local Congressperson complaining about the federal income tax code – the Internal Revenue Code.

There's a reason for this.

The Code, and its accompanying regulations, now contains more than 10 million words. Ten… million… words.

Your representative most likely makes a lot of noises about wanting it simplified and shortened.

And if you were to pay attention to the so-called "tax press," as I do, you'd also be aware of the grumblings and rumblings of the CPA and tax law communities – aka "tax professionals" – complaining, likewise, about how complicated and convoluted federal tax law is.

The Internal Revenue Code is littered – and I use the word "littered" intentionally – with baffling provisions that make even experienced CPAs and attorneys scratch their heads, policies that make elected representatives curse and refer to IRS employees as "jack-booted thugs" simply for enforcing what Congress has put in place.

Quite often, the Code doesn't make a lot of sense.

But don't be misled by the fact that tax professionals complain about the Code and Regulations so much. These rules are their bread and butter. The Code is the basis of how many of these folks make their collective living. If the Code and Regs were made significantly simpler, a lot of tax professionals might have to find another line of work.

By the same token, when your elected representatives scream and shout about the Code and Regs, keep in mind that they and the folks they've replaced over the last forty or fifty years have done very little to simplify them. In fact, it's just gotten bigger and bigger.

Taxes are tricky for the average person. I know this personally, and I can feel your pain.

When I was in school, I'd review my wimpy little Form 1040-EZ with its lone W-2 information a dozen or so times before sending it in, worrying over every line, checking and double-checking my math, crossing my fingers hoping that I hadn't made a mistake.

Since that time, I've worked at the Internal Revenue Service for more than 20 years, as a Tax Examiner, Revenue Officer and Tax Analyst. I've gotten to know the Internal Revenue Code and IRS procedure pretty well.

I wrote several thousand Technical Assistance responses to questions from the Austin Exam, Underreporter and Accounting functions. Whenever examiners or technicians were unsure about how the tax law should be applied in any number of scenarios, their questions and the related return data would be forwarded to me. My responses were basically legal opinions on the validity of these claims made by taxpayers. I saw thousands of different scenarios, and researched every one.

Prior to working for the IRS, I went to law school, got my Juris Doctorate degree, and passed a couple of bar exams.

When you start out in law school, one of the first things you're told by professors in orientation sessions is, "We're not here to teach you the law; we're here to teach you to think like attorneys."

So, in writing this book, I'm looking at tax law from three very different perspectives – as an attorney, as a former Revenue Officer, and as a taxpayer.

From the standpoint of an attorney, I'll point out what the tax law *is* in a given situation, or at least what it *appears* to be. (Hey, I'm the first to admit – tax law isn't always clear.)

From the outlook of Revenue Officers, the folks I'll refer to as "Auditors," I'll tell you what I think your average Auditor would do in a given scenario. Bear in mind that auditors come from all walks of life, and they're as different from one another as people you went to school with probably were.

And, as a taxpayer, I'm writing this in a way that I can easily understand, with the hope that you'll understand it, too.

Let me digress briefly and tell you a little bit about IRS employees, since these are the folks I hope this book keeps you from needing to deal with.

I've never met a single IRS employee who fantasized, when they were 12 years old, about auditing tax returns in the same way that, say, Michael Phelps dreamed of being an Olympic champion. And here's another little tidbit… relatively few IRS employees ever took so much as a single post-high school accounting class. Only a small percentage are CPAs or attorneys. I point this out only to demonstrate that these people probably aren't so different from you, so don't be intimidated by them, or by the income tax, itself.

Most IRS employees started working for the Service simply because they needed jobs. And you can count me as being one of those. Working for the IRS never even entered my mind when I was younger. It wasn't even remotely on my radar.

Once I started working there, however, I gradually became more and more intrigued with the interplay of different provisions of the Code. The IRC seemed to make sense most of the time… *most* of the time.

Hopefully, I can help make sense of the tax provisions that apply to rideshare for you.

Ridesharing or Contract Delivery as an Introduction to Entrepreneurship

Here it's probably important that I define ridesharing as it'll be discussed in this book. For our purposes, let's say that it's the practice of driving your personal vehicle for hire, using an online-based platform that connects drivers with passengers. Instead of flagging down a cab from the curb or calling a cab company, users can text a number, or, alternately request a ride via an app that they've downloaded to their phones. This app can also provide the user with a price quote for the trip, track the driver's location, and allow them to pay the fare using a credit card. In its current state, rideshare drivers are contractors, as opposed to employees, of the rideshare company. As contractors, they must pay their full portion of Social Security and Medicare taxes; regular salaried employees typically only pay half of these taxes, while their employer foots the other half of the bill. Contract employees, however, are able to deduct a much larger portion of their business expenses than salaried employees. Likewise with Contract Delivery drivers.

Being a rideshare driver is a hands-on introduction to entrepreneurship for many people. It's the opportunity to get the feel of running your own small business and see if it's for you... maybe it'll give you the itch to open up a different business in the future, doing something you love.

But it's also a quick immersion into the responsibilities of business. One of which is income taxes.

Hopefully, this book will give you the tools you need to confidently prepare your tax return as a rideshare driver.

The Value of Preparing Your Own Tax Return

As I said earlier, when I was putting together my first tax return, I was unnerved by the prospect. Even though I'd received only a miniscule amount of income on a single W-2, and all I had to file with the IRS was a Form 1040-EZ, I checked and rechecked my figures probably ten times. Then I signed it, put it in the mail, and hoped that everything went well. (Yes, my first return was filed on paper in the Dinosaur Age, before electronic filing was even an option.)

So I understand the anguish that can go into doing your own taxes.

That said, since you're reading this book, or at least previewing it through your eBook reader, you've most likely made the decision to do your own tax return. And unless you have some problematic issues unrelated to your rideshare income, I think self-preparation is a wise move. Why?

You'll get a more thorough idea of how your rideshare income and expenses work

The mere exercise of preparing your return gives you a magnified look at your business, from the top down.

Think of it this way. If you simply turn all your records over to a tax preparer, they'll probably ask you a number of questions and then set to work on your return. And when they've finished the return and handed it to you, you'll probably think, "Wow... I didn't think I'd owe that much." And, worse, you won't have learned anything about running a small business in a way that minimizes your taxes.

A little later on, I'll introduce you to self-employment income's "Rule of Seven." This bit of knowledge is a golden nugget I grasped early on when I was working as a Tax Examiner with the IRS.

A complete awareness of this rule will give you a much better perspective of how your self-employment deductions work, and how significant they actually are.

You'll keep control of your return in your own hands, rather than a preparer's

If having a preparer do your return will help you sleep better at night, then,

14

by all means, go for it. However, you won't have gained the knowledge I describe above.

Also, let's talk about preparers for a little bit. A majority – and, I mean, a *vast* majority – of preparers are very scrupulous and want to get your return absolutely right.

If you have a CPA prepare your return, you're pretty much golden, and there shouldn't be any reason to worry about your tax return. There's always the possibility of audit, no matter who prepares your return, but it's probably minimal. A CPA's services, however, can be expensive.

If you go to a "big-box" preparer – one of the big nationwide companies – you're still probably in good hands, although many of their preparers are employed on a seasonal basis, and aren't full-time tax professionals. However, these folks can charge you hundreds of dollars for just a simple return. When you throw self-employment income and self-employment tax into the mix, the price can increase significantly.

If you're opting for a local or independent preparer, do a little research, see if they've been in business awhile, and try to learn what their reputation is.

No matter which route you choose, if you choose *not* to prepare your return yourself... please, please, *please* perform some due diligence checks. At a very minimum, go online and check your local Better Business Bureau (BBB).

Pay special attention to what the BBB says, and search online with the particular preparer's name and the word "fraud" to see if anything adverse appears. Also be aware that there have been, and will most likely continue to be, fraudulent preparers out there associated with national chains. I'm not suggesting that certain chains are fraudulent but, as with anything, a few bad actors can spoil a company's reputation.

One type of fraudster might overstate your expenses or deductions, create false dependents or claim credits that you're not entitled to. Be certain to review the return before paying for it. Make sure that you understand why everything's on the return.

Another fraudster may hand you a paper return with correct figures and give you an immediate refund of the amount shown on your return – while eFiling a

15

return with inflated expenses or deductions or fraudulent credits, and pocketing the difference generated by an inflated refund. A year or so later your get a letter from a section of the IRS either known as "Exam" or "Underreporter," asking you where all these absurd figures came from.

Bear in mind – it doesn't matter whether you actively participated in the fraud or not. Even if the fraud was perpetrated by a preparer, you're the one ultimately liable for the actual tax owed.

Will this book help you "Audit-Proof" your tax return?

You may come across any number of tax guides, tax preparers or even tax preparation software that claim that their advice or service will allow you to "audit-proof" your return.

I make no such claim with this guide.

"Audit-proofing" implies that your return will not be audited by the IRS or your state taxing authority. I don't necessarily think that using the phrase is deceptive, but you'll often see an asterisk next to such claims that qualifies the phrase somewhere else, in much smaller print. No return is technically "audit-proof," and I won't mislead you by suggesting it. In this book, what you see is what you get. I'd like to think I'm a non-asterisky-kinda guy.

That said, the realistic odds of your return being audited are at historic lows. The 2015 Internal Revenue Service Data Book shows that the IRS audited 0.83 percent of all individual income tax returns filed in calendar year 2014 – roughly one of every 120 returns filed. That's a lot – it's more than *1.2 million* individual tax returns audited during that calendar year – but then consider that represents a *22% decrease* from 2010 enforcement figures.

Why has this number dropped so much? Budget cuts and the implementation of the Affordable Care Act over the last several years have limited the resources available to carry out enforcement – for our purposes here, audits. Consider that IRS staffing has decreased 16% since 2010 – and a whopping 32 % since 1992. You might guess that some of these personnel have been rendered unnecessary because of advancements in technology. That's true to some degree, but the drop also reflects Congress' desire to "punish" the IRS for some recent scandals, coupled with a willingness to let tax enforcement wither.

So what does this mean for you?

Simply that the likelihood of your return being selected for audit was extremely low several years ago, and it's even lower right now. And to be audited, a return generally has to have some disproportionate amount s of deductions or credits that are wholly out of whack with an "average" return with similar income.

17

This does not mean that you should take liberties with your return. Picture the level of tax enforcement as a pendulum that sways left and right. At the moment, the pendulum is well to the left, representing a relatively small percentage of audits. That pendulum will, at some point, swing back the other direction. It's been the historical norm.

You don't want to get into a mindset where it's okay to fudge on your taxes – number one, because you'll be in violation of federal law but, more practically, because you'll be more likely to get caught at some point in the future.

Bear in mind, also, that there's no statute of limitations when the IRS can establish that a taxpayer has filed a false or fraudulent return, willfully attempted to evade tax, or failed to file a return. When that pendulum swings back, you don't want it hitting you in the face.

If you've bought tax software to prepare your return, you'll probably be offered some type of audit support for an additional fee. Should you purchase this service? It may be worth the money if it eases any concerns you have about your return – you really can't put a price on peace of mind. But with the historically low audit rate we're now experiencing... your money might be better spent taking your significant other out to a nice dinner.

WHAT *NOT* TO SKIP WHILE READING THIS BOOK

If you're like me, you may not read how-to guides cover to cover. I'll admit it – I jump to the topics that seem most important to me, or the subjects that look the most interesting. I acknowledge, at least subconsciously, that I may be missing out on important information. But I think that most of us are busier than we might like, and we make decisions based on what we consider to be the most efficient uses of our time. This is just how our lives are.

That said, I'd strongly – *strongly* – urge you to look at

- **HYPOTHETICAL MILEAGE SCENARIO FOR DEDUCTIONS**
- **STANDARD MILEAGE RATE vs. ACTUAL CAR EXPENSES**
- **CAN I DEDUCT IT?**
- **MANAGING YOUR RIDESHARE BUSINESS**

HYPOTHETICAL MILEAGE SCENARIO FOR DEDUCTIONS sets up an example that I'll use several times throughout the book, particularly in the "CAN I DEDUCT IT?" section. In this hypothetical, I've calculated the mythical driver's business use of his vehicle to be 70%. Don't be confused into thinking that 70% is a magical percentage that should always be used in your own calculations. This is merely an imaginary situation, and you'll need to figure your own percentage of business use. The computation itself is simple – all you need to input is the total miles, personal and business, that you drove during the period that you've rideshared, and the miles driven during that period *specifically* for ridesharing. Just be aware that I'm using this hypothetical a number of times in the text.

STANDARD MILEAGE RATE vs. ACTUAL CAR EXPENSES is critical, especially if this is your first tax return to report rideshare income. As I'll show you, once you make a certain election, you're prohibited, by law, from taking inconsistent tax positions in subsequent years.

Here, I need to make a very important point. When claiming auto expenses, you usually have the option of claiming either Actual Car Expenses, or using the Standard Mileage Rate (I'll discuss these later.) The Standard Mileage Rate is considered to include certain items – gasoline and insurance, among others – so you can't claim those expenses when you're using the Standard Mileage Rate. That is, if you're claiming Standard Mileage, gasoline and insurance are already deemed to be included in that computation, so you can't claim them again, separately. In IRS parlance, claiming these items *in addition to* the Standard Mileage Rate would be considered "double-dipping" – taking the same deduction twice. Auditors see this time and again. It's always a no-no, and will earn you more than a hand-slap if your return is examined. If you should make such prohibited choices, your chances of being audited increase dramatically.

CAN I DEDUCT IT? This section probably addresses the main issues that induced you to buy this book, so you were probably going to look at this section, anyway. Here, I address three different questions – can an item generally be deducted, can it always be deducted, and where should it be deducted?

First, can a specific item generally be deducted? There are some items that an auditor or ethical tax professional would simply not allow you to claim as "ordinary and necessary." I'll point these out.

Second, if an item can *generally* be deducted, can it *always* be deducted?

And finally, when an item can be deducted, *where* should it be deducted? There's often more than one answer, depending on the nature of the item, and how you're choosing to deduct it.

If this section doesn't include a particular deduction that you want to claim, I'd suggest that you read the subsections, "A Deduction Must Be "Ordinary" and "Necessary"" and "Ward Cleaver and the Concept of Reasonableness." These should help you determine whether or not a certain expense is deductible or not.

MANAGING YOUR RIDESHARE BUSINESS describes some best practices that you, as a businessperson, should really consider. Some of them will help keep you out of harm's way with the IRS, others are simply good ideas for keeping your business well-organized.

INCOME ITEMS

Your rideshare company will probably send you, or make available to you online, IRS Form 1099-MISC, "Miscellaneous Income," *and/or* Form 1099-K, "Payment Card and Third Party Network Transactions." These are sent out early in the year and cover the previous year's income and expenses.

Form 1099-MISC

Technically, a rideshare company isn't required to issue a 1099-MISC unless a contractor – which would be you – has been paid at least $600 during the year.

What to report on Schedule C. Box 7 of Form 1099-MISC, "Nonemployee compensation," reports what you've earned as referrals, incentive payments, prizes, awards, and any other miscellaneous payments. Enter this amount on line 1 of Schedule C, "Gross receipts or sales."

Form 1099-K

On the other hand, a rideshare company isn't required to send you a 1099-K unless you've received more than 200 payment card transactions during the year through their service, *and* those transactions reflect gross payments over $20,000.

Box 1a of Form 1099-K, "Gross amount of payment card/third party network transactions" shows the money that's come into your hands via payment card transactions. This amount includes all third-party payments from passengers – gross fares, tolls, sales tax, city fees, airport fees, split fare fees and booking fees – with no fees for the rideshare company deducted.

The amount shown in Box 1a will generally be greater than the amount that the rideshare company has deposited into your bank account, since the amount deposited reflects the Box 1a amount, *minus* the rideshare company's fees.

What to report on Schedule C. Enter the amount from Box 1a on line 1 of Schedule C, "Gross receipts or sales" – the same place that you entered the Form 1099-MISC Box 7 amount.

Income Not Reported on a 1099-Series Form

If you don't receive a 1099-K or 1099-MISC, but you earned money from ridesharing, the income must still be reported as taxable income. Like payments reflected on the 1099s, this income is reported on line 1 of Schedule C, "Gross receipts or sales."

Income Not Reported to Your Rideshare Company

If you earned money that wasn't reported to your rideshare company – cash tips, for example – this likewise must be reported as taxable income, on line 1 of Schedule C, "Gross receipts or sales." You should keep a log of tips that you receive throughout the year, but which aren't paid via payment card.

AN OVERVIEW OF DEDUCTIONS

Generally, whether a deduction is allowable is fairly common-sensical – that is, for the most part, the rules are fairly logical and straightforward.

For example, if you use your car for both personal and business expenses, you can typically pro-rate a deduction, within IRS guidelines, to reflect only those expenses directly related to your business use of the car.

On the other hand, some deductions have extremely rigid guidelines that forbid pro-ration of any kind. The most extreme of these – which can be a red flag to the IRS if you claim a significant amount – is the Home Office Expense. If you use your home office for *any activity other than business*, you *cannot* take this deduction. However, if you follow the relevant rules – to a T – you may be able to claim expenses for your home office that you may not have even considered.

Before we move into what makes certain expenses deductible, let me touch briefly on a couple of basic issues.

Income Taxes vs. Self-Employment Taxes

You pay income tax based on your taxable income, which includes your self-employment income.

And, you pay self-employment tax based strictly on your self-employment income.

So you're really paying two different taxes when you work for yourself.

It's not a penalty on the self-employed. You just need to understand how the tax system works.

When you have a salaried job, you receive a Form W-2, Wage and Tax Statement, from your employer. You'd typically enter the amount from box 1 of the W-2, Wages, Tips, and Other Compensation, on line 7 of your Form 1040.

But, the amount in box 1 of your W-2 represents your base salary, *minus* your portion of Social Security and Medicare tax withheld – 7.65% of your salary (up to $118,500, at which point the rate drops to 1.45%.) This is paid into your Social Security and Medicare tax accounts. An equal amount, based on the same 7.65% rate, is paid into these accounts by your employer.

23

When you pay Self-Employment Tax on your self-employment income, the same thing is happening – that is, 7.65% is paid into your Social Security and Medicare accounts by both you and your employer. It just so happens that, as a self-employed taxpayer, you and your employer are one and the same, and you wind up paying the entire 15.3% into these accounts.

The "Rule of Seven"

This 15.3% rate is something to bear in mind when contemplating how valuable your deductions are. To compute SE tax, you multiply your net self-employment income by 15.3%... and *then* by .9235. This gives you a final self-employment tax rate of 14.13%, on amounts up to that magical $118,500 plateau, at which point the rate drops.

14.13% is almost exactly the percentage for the fraction one-seventh... an unwieldy fraction, to be sure, but an important one for our purposes.

One-seventh. If you take away nothing else from this book, take that fraction with you.

One-seventh represents a rough estimation of your self-employment tax. If your net self-employment income is $35,000, you can easily eyeball your SE tax as $5,000. (The actual computation comes out to $4,945, so you can see how close this estimation is.)

What this *also* means to you, though, is that, for every $7 of deductions you can find, your self-employment tax drops by $1.

If you have $7,000 of deductions, that's roughly $1,000 of self-employment tax that you save. If you have $14,000, that translates to roughly $2,000 of savings.

This is the "Rule of Seven."

Get it? The "Rule of Seven" applies until you reach that $118,500 plateau, at which point the rate drops, and it drops dramatically. Instead of saving $1 for every $7 of deductions, you'll save a dollar of SE tax for roughly every $37 of deductions. If you can reach this level, congratulations, you've done pretty darn well.

But the "Rule of Seven" is only one part of the equation.

The Reason that your Deductions are Doubly Important

This may be perfectly clear at this point, but I'll move forward, anyway. You pay self-employment tax on your self-employment income. But you pay income tax on your total income, which includes your self-employment income. So, any significant deductions you can take against your self-employment income will decrease not only your self-employment tax, but your income tax, as well.

Here's an illustration of how this plays out.

Let's say that you're single, your adjusted gross income is $40,000, your self-employment income is $20,000, you claim an exemption only for yourself, and you take the standard deduction. Your taxable income comes out to $29,650 and, based on the 2016 tax table, your tentative income tax is $3,988. Your Self-Employment tax – $20,000 multiplied by .153 by .9235 – is $2,826. So, your combined income tax and Self-Employment tax is $6,814.

NOW… let's assume that you documented your allowable self-employment deductions much better, or found deductions you didn't realize you were entitled to (which, hopefully, this book can help you find).

Let's say that you've found an additional $7,000 of deductions. The "Rule of Seven" tells us that this will yield us an SE tax decrease of roughly $1,000. In fact, the decrease in self-employment income from $20,000 to $13,000 drops SE tax by $989, from $2,826 to $1,837.

This brings your adjusted gross income down to $33,494. (The difference isn't exactly $7,000, because you have an adjustment for the self-employment tax deduction on page one of Form 1040. I explain this later, in the "Self-Employment Tax" essay in "CAN I DEDUCT IT?")

Based on this scenario, your taxable income has dropped to $23,144, yielding an income tax of $3,005, and your combined income tax and self-employment tax is now $4,842.

By finding $7,000 more in deductions, you've cut your combined taxes by almost $2,000. You've saved $1,972 – $6,814 minus $4,842.

This is a good concept to bear in mind when considering the compounded value of a deduction when you're self-employed. You've got not only the "Rule of Seven" working for you, but whatever your marginal tax rate is, as well.

This illustrates how essential it is that you recognize every deduction available to you.

Alright, enough of that. Now, on to what makes your expenses deductible.

A Deduction Must Be "Ordinary" and "Necessary"

According to the Internal Revenue Code, a business expense must be both ordinary and necessary to be deductible.

An ordinary expense is "one that is common and accepted in your field of business." That's fairly straightforward, right? If you were a carpenter, the IRS wouldn't bat an eye at your deduction for nails.

But what if you've come up with a novel idea that would actually help your business, an idea that's not mainstream? After all, some carpenter, somewhere, had to be the first to use a nail gun, right?

A necessary expense is "one that is helpful and appropriate to your business." Simple enough. But the IRS' interpretation, based on years and years of court rulings, is that an expense need not be "indispensable" to be considered "necessary." Yeah, you read that correctly. If you're like me, this makes no sense, on its face. "Necessary," to most of us, would mean much the same thing as "indispensable." So how does this work?

Here's an example that's relevant to ridesharing.

Let's say that you provide bottled water as a courtesy to your riders, and you want to deduct it as an expense on your tax return. Is this expense "ordinary," given the service you're providing? Moreover, is it "necessary?"

Auditors generally use all of the tools at their disposal to see how common an expense is. And, yes, this includes the internet. It wouldn't take long for a search to indicate that providing water isn't uncommon. So, we can say that bottled water is now an "ordinary" expense.

But let's say that ridesharing was in its infancy, and you were the first rideshare provider to be audited who claimed bottled water as an expense. You're Patient Zero, as it were. What's your argument to the IRS officer?

You'd explain to her how ridesharing works. If she pays any attention to the outside world, she'll know that you're reporting income received for providing a service, carting people around.

What she may *not* know is how you get your customers. You explain that, typically, rideshare providers receive ratings from their clients – and the higher your rating, the more opportunities you have to provide your service.

Do you think, at this point, the auditor will see where you're going with this argument? If not, spell it out – you provide bottled water, maybe satellite radio, maybe other small amenities, to get the highest possible ratings from your customers. You want your ratings to be better than those of other drivers to be offered more work opportunities – in other words, you're trying to gain a *competitive advantage*. And providing bottled water, bought in bulk, is a pretty cheap way to do it.

But if you think about this a bit further, you'll see that you've got another logical basis for the deduction. If you make bottled water available to the customer – even if the customer doesn't accept it – the likelihood of you receiving a tip goes way up. It's just an aspect of human nature that when someone offers you a kindness of some sort, no matter the size, it creates in you at least a subconscious desire to return the favor.

So, the expense is "ordinary." Is it "necessary?" We have to look at the IRS' definition of a "necessary expense" – it's one "that is helpful and appropriate to your business."

Could providing bottled water prompt or increase a tip? Yes.

Could providing bottled water increase your ratings? Yes.

Do higher ratings result in more offers to provide your service? Yes.

So… if offering bottled water can result in tips or more business opportunities, is that "helpful and appropriate to your business?"

Absolutely. You're giving yourself a competitive advantage by offering your additional service, and that's what all businesses strive to do. And, over time, a deduction that may not have necessarily started out as "ordinary" can evolve into one that is, simply because providers need to remain competitive to survive. It's economic Darwinism.

Ward Cleaver and the Concept of Reasonableness

Here's another way to think about it. Whenever you consider whether an expense is "ordinary" and "necessary," it might be useful to look at it through the lens of an IRS auditor – typically, a Revenue Officer or Revenue Agent – and view it in perspective of a different term – "reasonable." Is the deduction reasonable?

The key factor with any IRS folks who might examine your return, when it boils down to it, is the "reasonableness" of the expense. Providing bottled water to customers may not be ordinary or necessary using common-life definitions, but the auditor would most likely appreciate that this little perk makes business sense, and is therefore reasonable.

As a Revenue Officer with the IRS, I was occasionally confronted with issues that seemed to be of the first impression – that is, issues for which there was no precedent upon which to make a determination. Nothing written, anyway. I'd have to research IRS publications, the Internal Revenue Code, Regulations, external tax law databases… and still, sometimes, I'd just have to make a decision based on gut feeling.

This gut feeling was the concept of "reasonableness."

When I was in law school, professors would occasionally make reference to a "reasonable man" standard. They'd lay out some hypothetical scenario and ask, what would the "reasonable man" do?

Or… what would Ward Cleaver do?

Ward Cleaver was the father in the late 50s-early 60s sitcom, "Leave It To Beaver." This was classic "Americana" television, something that people seem to hark back to when they talk about "the good old' days." Sure, it seems quaint now, all white characters dealing with upper-middle class childhood problems. But such was TV back in the day.

Ward Cleaver was not always right – he'd misread his sons Wally and The Beav occasionally – but he was a kind man who always thought things through, and at the end of each episode he'd arrive at a rational and just decision, and occasionally a mild punishment.

That wasn't always easy with The Beaver around – poor Theodore was the child who seemingly never learned from his mistakes, making essentially the same bad decisions in one episode that he'd made two shows earlier. He got himself stuck in a billboard teacup, for crying out loud.

At any rate, the show was still in widespread syndication when I was in law school, and a lot of people had grown up watching. So it wasn't a great leap that the "reasonable man" was sometimes personified in Ward Cleaver. Most everyone knew who he was. "What would Ward Cleaver do?" became a mantra of sorts in law school. Invoking Ward Cleaver meant trying to be fair and equitable, doing the right thing.

It's also vaguely the standard that most Revenue Officers use, and it's something that you might bear in mind when you're weighing whether or not to claim a deduction. IRS employees are, by and large, reasonable people and, like you and me, they want to be right as often as possible.

The Varying Nature of Deductions

I'd be lying to you if I pretended that classifying deductions was the easiest thing in the world.

But I'd be doing you a further disservice if I made it harder than it has to be.

I really appreciate the quality of the publications that the IRS puts out. From time to time I worked with a number of people from "Forms and Pubs," and they strive to produce the best publications possible. These documents are generally as good as or better than whatever you might buy there on the open market... but, gosh darn it, you still have to slog through them in waders.

And it's not the fault of the folks at Forms and Pubs. They're trained to try to write at a certain grade level. But as much as they might try, simplifying the Internal Revenue Code for the average reader can be a nightmare.

So, here's my 200-word attempt to simplify deductions for you.

There are items that you can "expense" – that is, you can take a full deduction on your tax return for them, in the year of the expense.

There are other items that you can depreciate – generally items with a prolonged useful life, such as a car.

There are items that *can* be depreciated, but for which you might be able to claim as a total deduction in their first year of their business use – a so-called Section 179 Deduction.

And finally, similar to a Section 179 Deduction, there are also items with a "Special Depreciation Allowance," aka "Bonus Depreciation", that you can also take an additional first-year deduction for.

Easy peasy, right?

HYPOTHETICAL MILEAGE SCENARIO FOR DEDUCTIONS

I'm including a number of mileage-based scenarios in the following pages. For consistency and ease of computation, and I'll assume the following in each of these:

- You put 20,000 miles on your car during the year.

- 6,000 of these miles were for your personal use.

- 14,000 miles were driven in rideshare service – picking up and transporting your riders, and returning to your home base after transporting the passengers.

The math in this example above is pretty simple – the business use of your vehicle will have constituted 70% of the miles you put on it during the year. 14,000 divided by 20,000 is 70%.

When the amount of a deduction should be based on the business use of an item, I'll often use this hypothetical and the 70% rate.

But don't become confused and think that this is a standard percentage – this is merely the rate I'll be using in the many of the examples. You'll need to compute the business-use percentage based on your own driving for the year, naturally. Just plug the relevant percentage into the relevant computation, and you'll be golden.

Which miles are business miles?

You'll most likely receive a document from your rideshare company that reports "On-Trip" Mileage, or something to that effect. This represents only the actual miles driven while transporting passengers, which is probably all that your rideshare company is aware of. Be aware that you can also include miles you've driven while going to pick up a passenger, miles driven while waiting for rideshare requests, and miles driven back home after your last passenger was delivered.

But – the burden is on you to record all of this. A mileage tracker that you use religiously is therefore critical – and it's deductible on your tax return, as well. You can also find a sample paper log in Table 5-2 of IRS Publication 463, Travel, Entertainment, Gift, and Car Expenses.

31

STANDARD MILEAGE RATE vs. ACTUAL CAR EXPENSES

When you use a car you own for a business purpose, you have two options to claim your vehicle expenses: the Standard Mileage Rate, or the Actual Car Expenses system.

Whichever option you use, you'll need to know how many miles you put on the car for your business use during the year. You'll also need to know the *total* mileage – personal *and* business – that you drove your car during the year, since many deductions will be based on a ratio of business miles to total miles.

A lot of people choose the Standard Mileage Rate method as their default option, simply because it's easier. For this method, each mile you drive for your business is deductible at a rate of so many cents per mile. This mileage rate usually changes from year to year – and, occasionally, within a year – but in 2016, the rate was 54¢ per mile.

> *Example.* In our basic hypothetical, our driver put 14,000 business miles on her car in 2016. The Standard Mileage Rate was 54¢ per mile, so her deduction is $7,560.

With the Actual Car Expenses method, you add together all of the relevant expenses for your vehicle for the tax period in which the car has been used for your business, and pro-rate those expenses based on your rideshare mileage.

> *Example.* Using the same scenario, you put 20,000 total miles on your car last year, 14,000 of which were for your rideshare business. So, 70% of the miles were for business. Let's say that your actual expenses – and this includes one very theoretical item, depreciation – were $12,000. This means that your deduction was $8,400 – 70% of $12,000.

Which is the better option for you? Looking at this scenario, the Actual Car Expenses method would give you the larger deduction in this tax period – $8,400 to $7,560. Using the $8,400 figure would lower your net self-employment income by $840. This will not only lower your *income* tax, but also your *self-employment* tax. If you remember our "Rule of Seven," this $840 decrease will lower your SE Tax by roughly $120.

But should you opt for the Actual Car Expenses, even though it will lower your tax for this specific year? It's always best to crunch the numbers using each method, every year, but if this was your first year ridesharing, you need to be aware of...

The "First Year" Rule

Before we delve too far into the details of each of these methods, let's start with this significant little factoid: If you want to use the Standard Mileage Rate in *any* year for a car that you own, you *must* have chosen that option in the first year the car was available for use in your business.

The flip side of that coin: if you used the Actual Car Expenses method that first year, you're locked into using that same method every year after that.

At this point, you may be asking yourself – what happens if I use Actual Car Expenses the first year, but use the Standard Mileage Rate in a later one?

> *Example.* Mario claimed Actual Car Expenses when filing his first Schedule C for his ridesharing business. Because he didn't use the Standard Mileage Rate the first year his car was available for use in his business, he can't use the Standard Mileage Rate in subsequent years – he *has to use* the Actual Expenses Method from then on out. If he uses the Standard Mileage Rate, not only is he in violation of federal law, but his chances of being audited increase dramatically.

So what should *you* do the first year?

This is the major choice I cautioned you about earlier in the book. It's a big decision to make, and one that you don't want to make a rookie mistake on.

Let me emphasize one thing, however – the Standard Mileage Rate is *exponentially* easier to compute than the Actual Car Expenses Method.

As I suggested earlier, if you have the option of both methods, you should run the numbers for each one every year that you're ridesharing. But again, it's absolutely *critical* that first year.

If you're not sure which method to use on your initial rideshare return, or if the Actual Car Expenses amount isn't significantly larger that first year – and I mean, if it's not an *absolute blowout* – you're probably best served using the Standard Mileage Rate on the initial rideshare return. This will give you the opportunity to maximize your deduction in future years by using whichever method gives the larger benefit at that time.

Pros and Cons of Each Method

Assuming that both methods are available to you, you should run the numbers every year for each of these options to see what will benefit you most in that year. However, I can make these generalizations for each method.

Standard Mileage Rate

PROS:

- The Standard Mileage Rate method is much easier to compute than the Actual Car Expenses Method. Multiply your rideshare miles by the mileage rate, and that's basically it.
- Recordkeeping is extremely simple – just keep a log of your business miles. This used to be somewhat complicated… you'd have to keep an actual paper "log," track the miles on your odometer, and record the miles… assuming you remembered to do all that. Here in the third millennium, though, there are any number of apps available to make this process pretty much painless.
- If you used the Standard Mileage Rate the first year, you have the option of choosing whichever method gives you the higher deduction in later years.
- Using the Standard Mileage Rate generally gives you a better return if you have an older car, or a less expensive car. Why? Because depreciation, which is key in the Actual Car Expenses Method, will probably generate a smaller deduction for an older or less expensive car than what the Standard Mileage Rate will yield. (Bear in mind, this is a generalization and isn't always true.)

CONS:

- Conversely, using the Standard Mileage Rate will probably give you a lower deduction than Actual Car Expenses if you have a newer or more expensive car, which will probably benefit from a higher depreciation allowance.
- It will probably not provide the higher deduction in years when you have a lot of higher-dollar repairs or maintenance expenses.

34

Actual Car Expenses Method

PROS:

- Using Actual Car Expenses will probably yield a higher deduction if you have a newer or more expensive vehicle.
- This method will most likely give you a higher deduction in years when you've incurred high repair or maintenance expenses.
- A Section 179 Deduction or Special Depreciation Allowance, discussed later, is available the first year you place the vehicle in service for your rideshare business. These can give you a somewhat higher deduction in the first year you place a car into service.

CONS:

- The Actual Car Expenses option requires precise record-keeping of every possible expense. Not just large expenses like repairs and maintenance – to get the entire benefit, you'll need to keep all your receipts and record all of the expenses every time you buy gas, for example, or have your oil changed. Then you'll need to add up all the expenses and pro-rate them based on your business miles divided by your total miles driven for the year. It's not an impossible task, but you have to be extremely diligent in your efforts, or you'll miss out on potential deductions.
- If you elected the Actual Car Expenses option the first year your car was in service, you're not allowed to choose the Standard Mileage Rate in later years.
- If a Section 179 Deduction or Special Depreciation Allowance was claimed in the first year you placed your car into business service, not only are you not allowed to use the Standard Mileage Rate thereafter, but your subsequent depreciation amounts may be significantly lower.
- Although the possibility of a Section 179 Deduction or Special Depreciation Allowance the first year may sound really good, there's a strict limitation on how much you can deduct.

Okay, so those are the positives and negatives of each method. Now, let's move to the nuts and bolts. It's not really exciting stuff. Just hold your nose, dive in, and come up for air now and then.

The Standard Mileage Rate Method

Each year, the IRS announces mileage rates for the upcoming tax year. There are generally different rates for different types of costs – miles expended for business purposes, miles traveled for medical or moving reasons, and miles put on your vehicle while performing charitable services. For our purposes, all we care about is the business rate.

Occasionally, there'll even be separate mileage rates for different periods during the year – these are typically the result of significant spikes or drops in gas prices. However, as I noted earlier, the Standard Mileage Rate for business usage was 54¢ per mile in 2016, and that rate is valid for the entire year.

To see what kind of deduction this rate gives you, just by itself, think of our hypothetical scenario, in which you put 14,000 rideshare miles on your car. At 54¢ per mile, that's a Standard Mileage Rate deduction of $7,560. Considering the "Rule of Seven" I spoke of before, that's a tax break of roughly $1,080. (The actual calculation is $1,068.19, so you can see how spot-on the Rule of Seven is.)

Bear in mind that when you opt to use the Standard Mileage Rate for a particular tax year, you *cannot deduct* your Actual Car Expenses for that year, *except for* business-related parking fees and tolls, that part of the interest expense on a loan for your rideshare car that represents your business use of the car, and any personal property tax that might be related to the business use.

You can't deduct, for example, depreciation, any lease payments you make, any maintenance or repair expenses that are needed, gasoline or oil, insurance, or vehicle registration fees.

Why not? Because Congress intended that all of these expenses would be considered to be included in the Standard Mileage Rate.

I noted earlier that when you choose the Standard Mileage Rate the first year your car was available for use in your rideshare business, you could use either method in subsequent years... but if you used Actual Car Expenses in that first year, you were locked into using those actual expenses for all subsequent years.

And now let me lay another little rule on you: once you've filed your *initial* rideshare tax return using the Standard Mileage Rate, you can't amend *that first return* to change to the Actual Car Expenses method. Got it? That is, once you've made the Standard Mileage Rate choice on the first rideshare return that you file, you're stuck with *that choice, for that return.* (And it's probably a good thing, since that leaves your options open for later years.)

Example. Jim Bob got a late start on filing his first tax return that contained rideshare income and expenses, and used the Standard Mileage Rate because it was easier to compute. However, after this return was filed, he had time to go through all of his receipts and figure depreciation on his car. He discovered that the Actual Car Expenses method lowered his self-employment income – which meant that both his self-employment tax *and* his income tax would've been smaller. He can't amend the return he's already filed to claim his Actual Car Expenses. However, since he used the Standard Mileage Rate the first year, he'll be able to use either method in later years.

When you *can't* use the Standard Mileage Rate Method

There are several scenarios in which you're *not* allowed to use Standard Mileage, which I list below. The third through sixth circumstances below probably won't apply to your real-life situation, but I'll list them all in the interest of completeness.

You can't use the Standard Mileage option when you:
1. Have claimed a Section 179 Deduction on the car (also discussed later), *or*
2. Have claimed a special depreciation allowance on the car (again, discussed later), *or*
3. Have used five or more cars for business at the same time (and this *literally* means at the same time – at least five must have been used for business purposes in the same exact moment), *or*
4. Have claimed a depreciation deduction for a car using any method other than straight line depreciation – for example, the Modified Accelerated Cost Recovery System (MACRS, discussed later), *or*
5. Have claimed Actual Car Expenses after 1997 for a car you leased, *or*
6. Are a rural mail carrier who received a qualified reimbursement from the Postal Service.

Other Expenses you can claim when applying the Standard Mileage Rate

Although the Standard Mileage Rate is deemed to include certain expenses – for gas, oil, depreciation, lease payments, maintenance, repairs, insurance, and vehicle registration fees – it does *not* include the following expenses. That is, these can be claimed *in addition to* the Standard Mileage Rate.

Interest on car loans

As a self-employed rideshare provider who uses your car in your rideshare business, you can deduct the portion of the interest expense on a car loan that represents your business use of the car.

In our hypothetical example, we determined that 70% of the miles put on your car for the year were for business purposes. If the interest on your car loan was $1,000 for the year, then $700 would be deductible.

These expenses are deductible whether you use the Standard Mileage Rate or the Actual Car Expenses method.

Where to deduct: Line 16b of Schedule C, "Interest (Other)."

Personal Property Taxes

You have a couple of choices here, relating to personal property taxes on a car you used in your rideshare business.

If you're itemizing deductions on Schedule A (Itemized Deductions,) your first option is to write the entire amount off there, on line 7, "Personal property taxes."

More likely than not, however, the better idea is to deduct the business portion of state and local personal property taxes on a car used in your business on line 23 of Schedule C, "Taxes and licenses." (You can take this deduction whether you use the Standard Mileage Rate or the Actual Car Expenses method.)

In our hypothetical example, we determined that 70% of the miles put on your car for the year were for business purposes. If the interest on your car loan was $1,000 for the year, then $700 would be deductible on line 23 of Schedule C.

Then, if you itemize deductions using Schedule A, you can include the remainder of the state and local personal property taxes – and when using our hypothetical scenario, this would be $300 – on line 7 of Schedule A.

Why would you separate the amounts like this?

Simple. The deduction will lower your Adjusted Gross Income (and therefore, income tax) no matter where you claimed it.

However, if you claim the business-related portion on Schedule C, it also lowers your gross self-employment income, and therefore your self-employment tax, as well. Here, using our hypothetical example, the deduction on Schedule C lowered self-employment income by $700. And we know, using our "Rule of Seven," that this will lower self-employment tax by roughly $100.

Where to deduct: Line 23 of Schedule C, "Taxes and licenses," and, as appropriate, line 7 of Schedule A, "Personal property taxes."

Parking fees and tolls

Since parking fees and tolls are not included in the Standard Mileage Rate, you can also deduct any of these incurred while providing your rideshare service.

Where to deduct: Line 9 of Schedule C, "Car and truck expenses."

The Actual Car Expenses Method

If you don't use Standard Mileage Rate, you may be able to deduct the actual expenses for your car during the tax year. And again – if you're eligible to use either method, run calculations for both every year to see which benefits you more.

Actual Car Expenses include:

- Depreciation,
- Gas,
- Garage Rent,
- Insurance,
- Lease Payments,
- Licenses,
- Oil,
- Parking Fees,
- Registration Fees,
- Repairs,
- Tires, and
- Tolls.

When you've fully depreciated a car – that is, when its paper value for accounting purposes has dropped to zero – you can continue to claim your other actual car expenses in future years. At that point in time, it's possible that the car may no longer be acceptable to the rideshare service – that is, the terms of the agreement you signed with your rideshare company may require that the car you drive be a newer model – but if it still is, it's important to continue to maintain your records.

Business versus Personal Use of Your Car

As with the Standard Mileage Rate, you must keep track of the business miles you put on your car. When using Actual Car Expenses, however, you also have to keep track of the *total miles* you put on your car.

This isn't really all that difficult.

If you're ridesharing at the beginning of the year, note your beginning mileage on January 1, and pro-rate all expenses through the end of the year, or when you cease your ridesharing business.

If you begin ridesharing on, say, July 1st, note your mileage on that date, and pro-rate all expenses from that date through the end of the year, or when you cease your ridesharing business.

> *Example.* Marybeth has computed her Actual Car Expenses for the year to be $9,400. Using our hypothetical scenario from earlier in the book, she drove her car 20,000 miles during the year, 14,000 miles of which were for business. Her business use of the vehicle was 70% (14,000/20,000). Therefore, the amount of Actual Car Expenses that Marybeth claims on her Schedule C will be $6,580.

Interest on car loans

As a self-employed rideshare provider who uses your car in your rideshare business, you can deduct the portion of the interest expense on a car loan that represents your business use of the car.

In our hypothetical example, we determined that 70% of the miles put on your car for the year were for business purposes. If the interest on your car loan was $1,000 for the year, then $700 would be deductible.

These expenses are deductible whether you use the Standard Mileage Rate or the Actual Car Expenses method.

Where to deduct: Line 16b of Schedule C, "Interest (Other)."

The Section 179 Deduction, the Special Depreciation Allowance and the Depreciation Deduction

Brief Overview

When you use the Actual Car Expenses method, you can deduct not only the items detailed above, but these three rather theoretical deductions.

Very briefly... the Section 179 Deduction and the Special Depreciation Allowance are relatively large deductions that you're able to take the first year you place a vehicle into service. They're available to small business operators such as you, but these were passed into law mainly to give larger businesses more flexibility in cash flow, to help them try to keep their tax liability fairly constant over a period of years.

There might be the temptation to take the largest possible deduction you can during for first year of your rideshare business. You might want to consider doing otherwise, however. Taking these will lower the "basis" in your vehicle, and result in progressively smaller deductions in future years. This can result in not only higher income tax in future years, but higher self-employment tax, as well.

Depreciation, very simply, is a deduction that represents the loss in value of an item over time.

The Basics of Depreciation for Your Car

For depreciation purposes, a car is any four-wheeled vehicle, including a truck or van, with an unloaded gross vehicle weight of 6,000 pounds or less. It must be made primarily for use on public streets, roads, and highways. It includes any part, component, or other item physically attached to it or usually included in the purchase price.

Generally, the cost of a car, including sales tax and any improvements, is a categorized as a "capital expense" – a payment made by a business for, among other things, equipment such as automobiles. When the benefits of such an item generally last longer than one year, you typically can't deduct a capital expense – you have to depreciate it over time. Depreciation lets you recover the cost over more than one year, by deducting part of the cost each year to help offset income earned during that year. Passenger cars are generally depreciated over a five-year period.

There are typically limits on these deductions.

For example, special rules apply if the business use of your car is not more than 50% of its total use.

Also, if you used the Standard Mileage Rate the first year your car was placed in service for your business, you can't claim the Section 179 Deduction, or use any depreciation method other than a straight line method.

And, if you claim either a Section 179 Deduction or use other than a straight line depreciation method in the first year your car was placed in service for your business, you can't use the Standard Mileage Rate on that car in subsequent years. You have committed to using the Actual Car Expenses method as long as it's used in your business.

The Section 179 Deduction

The Section 179 Deduction lets you treat a portion of the cost of your car as a current expense. That is, it's an expense that can largely or entirely be deducted immediately, as opposed to being depreciated over time.

You need to note that there is a significant limit on the total Section 179 Deduction, special depreciation allowance, and depreciation deduction for cars that may minimize or completely eliminate any benefit you may receive by claiming the Section 179 Deduction.

When you make this election, you have to reduce your depreciable basis in the car by the amount of the Section 179 Deduction.

And for purposes of the Section 179 Deduction, the cost of the car does not include any amount figured by reference to *any other property* held by you, at any time. Most commonly, this means that if you used cash and a trade-in to buy a car for use in your rideshare business, then your "cost" for purposes of the Section 179 Deduction does not include the adjusted basis in the car you traded in for the new car. That is, your cost includes *only* the cash you paid. For Section 179 Deduction purposes, the trade-in never happened.

You're only allowed to take the Section 179 Deduction in the year that you placed the car in service. The IRS defines "placed in service" as "ready and available for a specifically assigned use, whether in a trade or business, a tax-exempt activity, a personal activity, or for the production of income." The IRS continues: "Even if you are not using the property, it is in service when it is ready and available for its specifically assigned use."

I'll point out here that there are a couple of Section 179 calculators online that might help you out. I don't want to name particular sites, but if you search "Section 179 Tax Deduction Calculator", you should be able to find them.

Be very careful here – a vehicle that you first used for personal purposes will not qualify for the Section 179 Deduction in a subsequent year, when you begin to use it for business.

Example. Aziz bought a new car in 2015. He didn't participate in rideshare that year, but used the car for personal purposes. Aziz started using the car for his ridesharing business in 2016. Since the car was "placed in service" in 2015 per the IRS' definition above, he can't claim the Section 179 Deduction in 2016 (or in any later year, for that matter). However, Aziz *can* claim depreciation for his business use of the car beginning in 2016.

More than 50% Business Use requirement

To claim a Section 179 Deduction, the business use of the car must be more than 50% of its entire use. When this is the case, all you need to do to determine the maximum Section 179 Deduction is multiply the cost of the car by the percentage of its business use. However – as I noted earlier, there is a limitation on depreciation, Section 179 Deduction, and a special depreciation allowance that can significantly reduce this potential deduction. See Appendix 3, Maximum Depreciation Deduction for Cars.

> ***Example.*** Cassie bought a new car in July 2015 for $26,500, and used 70% of its total miles for her rideshare business. Based on this usage, the portion of the cost of her car that qualifies for a Section 179 Deduction is $18,550. However, the limitation mentioned above will significantly limit the total deduction that Cassie can claim, down to $7,812. (I'll show you the computation a little later.)

If your car's business use was 50% or less of its total use, you cannot claim the Section 179 Deduction.

> ***Example.*** Reggie bought a new car in July 2015 for $14,600, but used only 45% of its total miles in his rideshare business. Reggie can't take a Section 179 Deduction, but the car is still eligible for normal depreciation.

Let's push the envelope, here, because someone, somewhere, will have the scenario in which *exactly 50%* of a car's miles were for business use. Could that someone claim the 179 Deduction? NO! To quote from the IRS' Publication 463: "You must use the property *more than 50%* for business to claim any section 179 deduction." (Emphasis mine.)

Limits

There are a number of limitations that relate to the Section 179 Deduction. I include the whole list, pulled straight from IRS publications, in the appendices at the end of this book.

However, for the vast majority or rideshare drivers, the only relevant limitation is the limit on the sum of your Section 179 Deduction, special depreciation allowance, and depreciation deduction.

Generally speaking, the maximum amount that you can claim for a car that is qualified property placed in service in 2016 is $11,160.

What does this $11,160 represent? Does this mean that Cassie, in our example above, can only deduct $11,160, rather than $18,550?

No! This $11,160 would be the maximum amount of Section 179 Deduction, special depreciation allowance and depreciation deduction – *combined* – if the car was used *100% for business.* When it's less than 100%, the amount is reduced proportionally. See Appendix 3, Maximum Depreciation Deduction for Cars.

> ***Example.*** In Cassie's hypothetical, above, she bought a new car in July 2015 for $26,500, and used 70% of its total miles for her rideshare business. Based on this usage, the cost of her car that qualifies for a Section 179 Deduction is $18,550 – that's $26,500 x 70%. *However* ... the total of her Section 179 Deduction, special depreciation allowance, and depreciation deduction is limited to $7,812 – that's the $11,160 maximum, multiplied by Cassie's 70% business use. This example should demonstrate that the Section 179 deduction isn't all it's cracked up to be, at least as far as cars are concerned.

How the Section 179 Deduction affects the "Basis" of your car, for depreciation purposes

The amount of the Section 179 Deduction reduces your basis in your car. If you elect the Section 179 Deduction, you must subtract the amount of the deduction from the cost of your car. The resulting amount is the basis in your car you use to figure your depreciation deduction.

> ***Example.*** Let's say that Cassie took a $6,000 Section 179 Deduction. Her basis for depreciation, then, will be $20,500 – the $26,500 purchase price, minus her $6,000 Section 179 Deduction.

When to make the choice

If you want to take the Section 179 Deduction, you must make the choice in the tax year you place the car in service for business or work. Again – you have to take it that first year, and you can *only* take it first year.

How to make the choice

Use Form 4562, Depreciation and Amortization, and file it with either your original Form 1040 filed for the year the property was placed in service (whether or not you file it timely), or with a timely-filed amended return.

When you make an election on an amended return, be sure to specify the item of Section 179 property that the election applies to, and the portion of the cost of each item to which it's relevant. The amended return must also reflect any adjustments to your taxable income that result from these changes.

As with all of your income and deductions, be sure to keep good records. For Section 179 purposes, retain documentation that identifies each piece of qualifying Section 179 property. These records need to show how and when you acquired the property, the person you acquired it from, and when you placed it into service.

Revoking the election

An election (or any specification made in the election) to take a Section 179 Deduction for 2016 can be revoked without IRS approval, simply by filing an amended return.

Why might you want to revoke this election? One very good reason is the potential, perhaps the likelihood, that you'll have to "recapture" the deduction in a later year. So-called "driverless cars" may become a reality soon, possibly putting a lot of rideshare drivers out of business.

When your business use of the car drops to 50% or less

Okay, this gets kind of ugly, so bear with me. It sounds worse than it actually is, and I'll provide an example to demonstrate. And bear in mind that if you use mass-market software to prepare your return, most of the heavy lifting will probably be done for you if you just plug in the right numbers.

To have claimed the Section 179 Deduction, you must have used the car more than 50% for business purposes *in the year you acquired it.*

If, in a *subsequent* tax year, your business use of the car winds up being 50% or less... (wait for it) ... you have to *recapture* any excess depreciation in that later year.

Uh... yeah. So, what, exactly, does this mean? It means that you have to include "any excess depreciation" in your gross income, and "add it to your car's adjusted basis for the first tax year in which you do not use the car more than 50% in qualified business use."

47

To figure the recapture amount, you must first compute the depreciation that would have been allowable *on the Section 179 Deduction you claimed*, starting with the year the property was placed in service, and including the year of recapture. Then, subtract this amount from the Section 179 Deduction you actually claimed. This is the amount you have to report as recapture.

What this calculation is doing, basically, is eliminating the benefit originally received by claiming the Section 179 Deduction, and replacing it with the depreciation he would've received on the 179 Deduction amount. (I explain the depreciation rates used below in the subsection "The Depreciation Deduction.")

Example. In January 2014, Jim Bob paid $24,000 for a new car and began using it immediately for his new rideshare business. He elected a $6,000 Section 179 Deduction for the car, and elected not to claim a special depreciation allowance (more on that later). He used the property 70% for business in 2014, 60% for business in 2015, and 40% for business in 2016. Here's how he figures his recapture amount.

Section 179 deduction claimed (2014) **$6,000.00**

Minus Jim Bob's allowable depreciation using the five-year depreciation rate (shown in Table A-1 of IRS Publication 946, How To Depreciate Property):

2014 . . . . $840.00

($6,000 x 70% business usage x 20.00% first-year depreciation rate)

2015 . . . . $1,152.00

($6,000 x 60% business usage x 32.00% second-year depreciation rate)

2016 . . . . $460.80

($6,000 x 40% business usage x 19.20% third-year depreciation rate)

MINUS the Total **$2,452.80**

2016 – RECAPTURE AMOUNT $3,547.20

So, Jim Bob has to include $3,547.20 in income for 2016.

He'll use Form 4797, Sales of Business Property, to report this amount.

In column (a) of line 33 of Form 4797, "Section 179 expense deduction or

---

48

depreciation allowable in prior years," he'll enter "$6,000.00."

In column (a) of line 34, "Recomputed depreciation," Jim Bob will enter "$2,452.80."

And in column (a) of line 35, "Recapture amount," he'll enter the recapture amount, $3,547.20.

Since Jim Bob originally would've claimed the Section 179 Deduction on Schedule C, he'll need to transfer the recapture amount there. It should be entered on line 6, "Other income, including federal and state gasoline or fuel tax credit or refund." And if line 31 of Schedule C shows a net profit, Jim Bob will need to enter the line 31 amount on line 2 of Schedule SE, "Self-Employment Tax." (The recapture amount is subject to self-employment tax, since the original Section 179 Deduction claimed on Jim Bob's initial Schedule C would have reduced (or possibly eliminated) his self-employment tax that year.)

Okay, so that's how recapture works when the business use of your car drops to or below 50%. But what happens if and when you sell the car? As you might guess… there's a tax consequence of doing that, too.

Sale of your car

If you should dispose of your vehicle, you might have to report a taxable gain, or you may even be able to claim a loss. The portion of any gain on the disposition that's attributable to depreciation, including a Section 179 Deduction or clean-fuel vehicle deduction (more on that later), and special depreciation allowance you claimed on the car will need to be treated as ordinary income. However, you may not have to recognize a gain or loss if you dispose of your car due to a casualty, theft, or trade-in.

To compute whether the sale of your car qualifies for a business loss or must be reported as a business gain, it's helpful to look at two strictly separate issues – your business use of the car, and your personal use of the car. You want to look at both of these uses because, while a business loss is deductible and a personal loss isn't, both a business gain *and* a personal gain would be included in income.

Example. Let's use our hypothetical scenario in which the car has been used 70% for business purposes each year, when Joaquin decides to sell his car. (In the likely event that your business use percentage varies each year, simply add up all of the business miles for the period during which you provided rideshare services, and divide those miles by total miles driven during the same period.)

Joaquin purchased a vehicle for $25,000. Based on 70% business use, his business basis of the car would have been $17,500, and his personal basis, $7,500. Easy so far.

During the tax period in which he used the car for business purposes, Joaquin claimed $8,547 in depreciation. Since depreciation only affects his business basis and not his personal use, this leaves him with a business basis of $8,953 – $17,500 minus $8,547.

Let's say that Joaquin sells the car for $11,000. His business portion of the sales price would be $7,700 – that's $11,000 x his 70% business use. This leaves him with a business loss of $1,253. Meanwhile, his personal portion of the sales price would be $3,300; when you subtract out his personal basis of $7,500, his personal loss would be $4,200.

The personal loss isn't deductible; if there were a personal gain, this would be reported in Part II of Form 4797, Sales of Business Property.

Joaquin's business loss – $1,253 – is reported in Part I of Form 4797, as would be any business gain from the sale of the vehicle.

Special Depreciation Allowance (aka "Bonus Depreciation")

You might be able to claim a special depreciation allowance for your car if it's a "qualified car" (defined below) and it was placed in service in 2016. This allowance is an additional depreciation deduction for 50% of the car's depreciable basis (that is, *after* any Section 179 Deduction you're going to claim, but *before* figuring your regular depreciation deduction under the MACRS scheme).

As with the Section 179 Deduction, this allowance applies only to the first year that your car is placed in service. Likewise, to claim the allowance, the allowance, more than 50% of the car's use must be for business.

Combined depreciation

The combined depreciation amount that you're allowed for a car in its first year– that is, your Section 179 depreciation, special depreciation allowance, and regular depreciation, *combined* – is limited to $11,160 for passenger cars. (See Appendix 3, Maximum Depreciation Deduction for Cars, for all relevant amounts.)

However, if you *only* depreciate the vehicle, or if you depreciate it and claim the Section 179 Deduction, the maximum amount you can claim is $3,160.

Clearly, if you want the biggest first-year write-off, you'll probably want to use the special depreciation allowance. The fact is, however, that as a small business, it will probably be in your best interests to be able to spread out your depreciation for as long as you use the car in rideshare.

The relevant amounts for trucks and vans are $11,560 and $3,560, respectively.

What's a Qualified Car?

To be a qualified car, three conditions need to be satisfied. You have to have purchased the car new, on or after January 1, 2008, but only if no binding written contract to acquire the car existed before January 1, 2008. You must have place it in service for your rideshare business before January 1, 2017. And finally, you must have used it more than 50% for your business.

You don't have to claim the special depreciation allowance

As I noted above you may want to spread depreciation over the life of your rideshare vehicle.

Why? Remember – you not only want to minimize your income tax, but your self-employment tax, as well. If you maximize deductions your first year, you decrease both your income and self-employment taxes that year. But in future years, the deduction you'll be able to claim will be much smaller, resulting in higher income and self-employment taxes.

If you don't want to claim the special depreciation allowance, you'll need to attach a statement to your *timely-filed* tax return (including extensions), indicating the class of property you're making this election for (which, for cars, is five years), and also stating that you're are electing *not* to claim the special depreciation allowance for qualified property placed in service during the tax year ending December 31, 2016. For a sample of this language see Appendix 2, Election not to claim the special depreciation allowance.

Unless you elect *not to claim* the special depreciation allowance, you'll need to reduce your car's adjusted basis by the amount of the allowance, even if it wasn't claimed.

The Depreciation Deduction

Depreciation is a fiction of sorts. It's an accounting slight-of-hand that originated a couple hundred years ago, used generally for longer-lasting items. Depreciation allows you to claim deductions over several years for the gradual decline in value of a capital asset – such as a car – that's expected to last for an extended period. It assigns a value on many long-lasting, generally larger-ticket items at varying points over time.

The amount of depreciation you claim over the years for an item will theoretically equal the replacement cost of that item when it has finally lost its value. The theoretical loss in value over the course of a single tax year is what you claim as depreciation for that year – *if* you can claim it.

CAUTION!!! If you claim depreciation or a Section 179 Deduction on your car the first year that you put it into service for rideshare, you can't use the Standard Mileage Rate in later years – you're tied to the Actual Car Expenses method from then on. (See STANDARD MILEAGE RATE vs. ACTUAL CAR EXPENSES.)

The kinds of property that you can depreciate include machinery, equipment, buildings, vehicles, and furniture. It may seem obvious to point out, but you can't take depreciation on property that you hold for strictly personal purposes.

When you use property for both business and personal purposes, you can only depreciate the portion used for business. That's one reason that keeping a correct mileage count is important.

To depreciate property, the property must:

- Be property you own (as opposed to lease), *and*
- Be used in a business or income-producing activity, *and*
- Have a determinable useful life, *and*
- Be expected to last more than one year, *and*
- Not be excepted property. Excepted property includes certain intangible property, certain term interests, and property placed in service and disposed of in the same year. This clause shouldn't affect you, but for more information, see IRS Publication 946, "How to Depreciate Property."

53

And, for your purposes, you can only deduct depreciation on your rideshare vehicle if you deduct your Actual Car Expenses, as opposed to using the Standard Mileage Rate.

What is "Basis?"

For depreciation purposes, "basis" is typically the car's cost. It includes the total of any amount you borrow, any amount you pay in cash, and any other property or services exchanged for the vehicle.

Generally, you figure depreciation on your car using your "unadjusted basis". This is typically your car's cost (including sales taxes, dealer preparation and destination charges; PLUS, any substantial improvements you've made to the car; MINUS, any Section 179 Deduction, any Special Depreciation Allowance, any gas guzzler tax, and any alternative motor vehicle credit you've claimed on the vehicle.

When you change the use of your car from personal to business – a very common scenario for rideshare drivers – then, your basis for depreciation is *the lesser of* fair market value of the car, or your adjusted basis in the car, on the date of your car's conversion to business use.

Let's say that your car was worth $26,845 when you put it into use for rideshare. This might've been the price you paid for it new, and you immediately started ridesharing. Or, if you had the car for a while before offering rideshare services, it might have been the "Fair Market Value" (FMV) when you started the service. This is an important value to know, because if you didn't start ridesharing with a brand-spanking new car, it's the amount that you base depreciation on.

The IRS has a rather clunky definition for FMV: it's "the price that property brings when it is offered for sale by one who is willing but not obligated to sell, and is bought by one who is willing or desires to buy but is not compelled to do so."

If you've had your car for a while when you start ridesharing and aren't sure what the FMV is, just click over to one of the used-car sales sites and run a query reflecting the make, model, year and condition of your car to see a range of prices for available cars in your area. DOCUMENT THIS RESEARCH –

save this data to a pdf or print it off. You'll need to arrive at a reasonable value – a "Fair Market Value" – of the car based on this range of prices, and you'll use that figure as the "basis" of your depreciation. It also wouldn't hurt to take photos of the car when you've made this search, which will back up your claim should you be audited.

Alternatively, you could actually get an estimate of your car's value from one of the big-chain used car dealerships in your area. These are typically fairly reliable and consistent. Again, document their offer.

When is the car considered to be placed in service?

Generally, this is when it's available for use in your business or for your personal activities. Depreciation begins when the car is placed in service for use in your business.

If you initially used the car only for your personal purposes and later began using it for rideshare, the car is considered to have been place into service on the date you started using it for rideshare.

If you've placed your car in service and disposed of it in the same tax year, you can't claim a depreciation deduction for it.

Available Depreciation Methods

Cars are typically depreciated using a five-year "recovery period." This is potentially misleading, however. It generally takes at least six years to fully depreciate a vehicle. The yearly allowable depreciation deduction for a passenger automobile is limited to a specific dollar amount each year and, because these limits are relatively low, it can take more than five or six years to fully depreciate your vehicle. (See Appendix 3, Maximum Depreciation Deduction for Cars, for the relevant limitations for each year the vehicle is in use.)

There are actually a few different methods through which you can depreciate your car. If you use a software program in figuring your taxes, it should allow you the option you want to use. And if you use the same software year after year, tracking what's already been claimed as depreciation should be automatic.

For more information, I'll point you to IRS Publications 946, "How To

55

Depreciate Property," and 463, "Travel, Entertainment, Gift, and Car Expenses," both available at www.irs.gov. It wouldn't be efficient for me to attempt to summarize depreciation for you – Pub 946, alone, is more than 100 pages long – but I'll provide a very quick overview.

The default depreciation system is known as "MACRS" – the Modified Accelerated Cost Recovery System. MACRS is a fusion of several depreciation methods. For cars, it allows 20% depreciation the first year; 32% the second; 19.2% the third year; 11.52% in each of the fourth and fifth years; and the remainder, 5.76%, in the fifth year. This method allows you to claim larger deductions in the early years of a product's use, but the rates drop as the car ages. (These figures can be found in Table A-1 of Publication 946, "3-, 5-, 7-, 10-, 15-, and 20-Year Property Half-Year Convention.")

It's important to realize that you can only claim depreciation in relation to the business use of your car.

Example. Jamaal has a car with a value of $26,845 when he places it into use for rideshare. His business use of the car was 70% the first year. Using the default depreciation system, and assuming that Jamaal is using the Actual Car Expenses method for his car, his deductible depreciation for that first year would be $3,758.30 – that's $26,845 x the 20% depreciation rate x his 70% business use of the car. The next year, assuming the same 70% business use of his vehicle, his deduction would be $6,013.28 – that's $26,845 x 32% x 70%. And so on.

Jamaal could also use what's known as the Straight-Line method.

Example. For his car, he could deduct 20% for each of the five years of his car's depreciable life. So, for a car with a value of $26,845, his deduction each year would be calculated by multiplying the business-use percentage of the car by $5,369 – that's 20% of the car's value when it was placed into rideshare service. His first year's depreciation deduction, in the 70% business use scenario, would be $3,758.30 – $26,845 x the 20% depreciation rate x his 70% business use of the vehicle.

Also note that the Straight-Line method is the one you'll have to use if you switch from using the Standard Mileage Rate on your tax return one year, to the

Actual Car Expenses system the next.

Then there's what's known as the 200% Declining Balance, or Double Declining Balance, method. Here, the bulk of the depreciation associated with an item is claimed in the early years of its use. In essence, this method shifts some tax liability from the early years of an item's use to later years, which may or may not be a good strategy for you. The Double Declining Balance method multiplies the Straight-Line depreciation rate by two, and then by the book value of the item – and that's the book value at the beginning of each year, *not* the original value when it was put into use.

Finally, there's a variation on the 200% Declining Balance system – the 150% Declining Balance method. Obviously, the initial amount of depreciation isn't quite as large as with the 200% method, but the amount you can claim in later years is larger.

Which of these methods is best for you? That depends on your whole income situation, beyond just your rideshare income, and also on whether you're eligible for any credits against tax. For example, if you're a student and are eligible for education credits, this might weigh into your decision. It's pretty complex stuff.

If you use income tax software, you should be able to try each method before submitting your return. This will give you a better idea of what your numbers will look like.

How to Depreciate when you used the Standard Mileage Rate in your car's first year of business use

If you elected the Standard Mileage Rate option in that first year, you'll have to use Straight-Line Depreciation for any subsequent years in which you use the Actual Car Expenses method.

To compute depreciation under the Straight-Line method, you'll have to reduce the basis in your car, but not to below zero, by a set rate per mile for the years in which you used the standard mileage rate. The per-mile rate generally changes from year to year, but not always.

Since 2009, the rates have been:

Years	Depreciation Rate per Mile
2010	$.23
2011	$.22
2012-2013	$.23
2014	$.22
2015	$.24

You'll notice that these rates are significantly lower than what was used in each of these years for the Standard Mileage Rate. That's because the amounts I list above are deemed to be only the depreciation portion of those mileage rates.

Then, you use the Straight-Line method over the remaining estimated useful life of your car.

Example. In 2014, Timmy bought a car for $19,800. He used it *exclusively* for business in 2014 and 2015, and used the Standard Mileage Rate in both of those years. He drove the car 16,200 miles in 2014 and 18,500 miles in 2015. In 2016, Timmy has very large expenses on his car, and decides to change to the Actual Car Expenses method for that year. To compute his depreciation for 2016, he'll need to figure his car's adjusted basis at the end of 2015.

In 2014, Timmy drove 16,200 miles for business. At 22¢ per mile, his depreciation in 2014 was $3,564.

In 2015, he drove 18,500 miles for business. At 24¢ per mile, his depreciation in 2015 was $4,440.

So, Timmy's basis in the car at the beginning of 2016 was $11,796 – his original basis ($19,800) minus his depreciation for 2014 and 2015 ($3,564 + $4,440).

Although cars are a five-year property for depreciation purposes, Timmy is allowed to estimate the remaining useful life of his vehicle and use Straight-Line Depreciation based on that. Timmy estimates that his car has a remaining useful life of four years, so he uses $2,949 ($11,796 ÷ 4) as his Straight-Line Depreciation amount for 2016. He then deducts his additional Actual Expenses, whatever those may have been.

Remember – you can't depreciate your car when you used the standard mileage rate in the first year of its business use, and changed over to the Actual Car Expenses method in a later year. You have to use straight line depreciation instead.

CAN I DEDUCT IT?

AAA or Other Motor Club Membership

How much of the expense can be deducted? Only deduct the amount that corresponds to the percentage of the car's use that was devoted to business. After all, your car can break down during your personal use, too. In our Hypothetical Mileage Scenario for Deductions, our imaginary driver used his car 70% for rideshare use. If his annual fee for membership in the motor club was $100, then $70 would be deductible.

Where to deduct: Line 27a of Schedule C, "Other expenses (from line 48)." Also include a description and the amount of the expense in Part V of Schedule C. If you need to list more than nine items in Part V and you're filing a paper return, include the first eight items in Part V, and indicate "See attachment" on the last line. Then, attach an additional document listing the remaining deductions. (If you're using tax software, additional lines will be able to populate, or the software will automatically create and title an appropriate attachment.)

Accountant, CPA or Other Tax Professional Fees

I'm hoping that this book will give you the confidence to prepare your own return that includes your rideshare income and deductions. As I argue in "The Value of Preparing Your Own Tax Return" section, I think that you'll gain a lot by preparing your own return – it's helpful to see how income and expenses interact, and to see how your own decisions can benefit you, tax-wise.

However, if you still feel the need to have your return prepared by a professional (at which point, this portion of the text theoretically becomes moot), the portion of your return that's related to your self-employment income is deductible.

How much of the expense can be deducted? This expense isn't tied to the number of business miles you've put on your car during the year, but the business portion of the expense should be readily identifiable.

A tax professional will normally provide a fee schedule for each portion of the return – for example, let's say a preparer charges $200 for a basic Form

1040, $100 for each Schedule C (where you figure your net business income or loss), and $50 for a Schedule SE (on which your self-employment tax is computed). Assuming that you have only a ridesharing business for your self-employment income, you can deduct the cost of your Schedule C and your Schedule SE – $150 – as a business expense.

Be aware that you can also claim the remainder of this fee – your personal income tax portion of the return preparation – on Schedule A as an Itemized Deduction. So what's the difference, you may be thinking. A deduction on Schedule A reduces your taxable income, and your income tax. A deduction on Schedule C, on the other hand, reduces not only your taxable income and your income tax, but also your self-employment tax. And remember our "Rule of Seven" – generally, every $7 that you can reduce your self-employment income will reduce your self-employment tax by $1.

And, just a personal tip – before you run out and hire a tax professional, I'd strongly suggest that you check with your area Better Business Bureau to find established, reputable businesses. Most preparers are absolutely trustworthy, but there are also scammers out there. Just be wary.

Where to deduct: There are actually different places where tax preparation expenses should be claimed – one spot for the business portion, and another for the non-business portion.

You can deduct the business-related part of your tax preparation expenses – in the example above, it's $150 – on line 17 of Schedule C, "Legal and professional services."

You can deduct the non-business-related portion – $200 in the above scenario – on line 22 of Schedule A, "Tax preparation fees." To get the benefit of this portion of the expense, however, the total of your itemized deductions on Schedule A would need to exceed the standard deduction that you'd otherwise claim.

Accounting Software

How much of the expense can be deducted? Similar to the expenses you might pay for a tax professional, you can deduct this expense only to the extent that it was used for purposes of your business. It's possible that this could be

100%, if you only used it for business purposes.

Where to deduct: Line 13 of Schedule C, "Depreciation and section 179 expense deduction," via Form 4562, "Depreciation and Amortization."

Please note that you can either depreciate this software over a three-year period, or expense the entire amount on your current return as a "Section 179 Deduction."

An accounting program would be an example of software with a three-year depreciation period. You're also now allowed to claim a Section 179 Deduction, described earlier, for off-the-shelf software, which allows you to claim a one-time expense for the entire purchase price, as opposed to depreciating it over the three year period. This would be easier, certainly, but if you use the same tax software over a period of years, the software should track yearly depreciation for you.

For software that needs to be updated frequently, you can enter updates you pay for in a number of places. Some advisors suggest line 23 of Schedule C, "Taxes and licenses," for the fees paid for licensing/renewing the software. Personally, I'd claim these expenses on either line 18, "Office expense," or line 27a, "Other expenses."

Software for which you have to purchase a subscription could go on any of these lines.

Treat state and local sales taxes as part of the cost of the software; do not deduct these taxes separately on line 23 of Schedule C, "Taxes and licenses."

Advertising

Rideshare drivers can generally advertise their services, as long as the communication doesn't violate any local laws.

How much of the expense can be deducted? All of it.

Where to deduct: Line 8 of Schedule C, "Advertising."

Bank Charges

How much of the expense can be deducted? Any fees associated with a separate rideshare account are deductible. This includes costs for check printing, check-writing fees and credit card fees associated with your business.

Similarly, any rideshare-specific expenses generated on a personal account would likewise be deductible. (But, *please* see the "MANAGING YOUR RIDESHARE BUSINESS" section, where I suggest that you set up separate accounts.)

Where to deduct: Line 18 of Schedule C, "Office expense."

Books, Magazines and Other Publications

The cost of books, magazines, newsletters and other publications that are relevant to the rideshare business are deductible. But bear in mind the "reasonableness" standard that I wrote about in the "Ward Cleaver and the Concept of Reasonableness" section. These publications must be rideshare-specific. For example, a subscription to "Car and Driver" probably won't cut the mustard, but if you bought a copy of "Car and Driver" on the newsstand with an article specific to the rideshare business, you're safe in taking that deduction.

Where to deduct: Line 18 of Schedule C, "Office expense." Treat state and local sales taxes as part of the cost of the publications; do not deduct them separately on line 23 of Schedule C, "Taxes and licenses."

Business Cards

This is a legitimate expense, as long as the cards promote your rideshare business. Including your passenger referral code would probably seal the deal for an Auditor, should you be so unlucky to have to deal with one.

How much of the expense can be deducted? As long as the cards provide your rideshare information (especially your referral code), this expense is fully deductible.

Where to deduct: Line 27a, "Other expenses." Treat state and local sales taxes as part of the cost of your business cards; do not deduct them separately on line 23 of Schedule C, "Taxes and licenses."

63

Car Expenses

See the "STANDARD MILEAGE RATE vs. ACTUAL CAR EXPENSES" section.

Car Insurance

See "Rideshare Insurance," later.

Car Washes and Detailing

This expense can be deducted whether you use the Standard Mileage Rate or the Actual Car Expenses method.

Don't go crazy when it comes to claiming a large expense for "detailing" – remember, if you're audited, the burden is on you to prove that an expense is both ordinary and necessary. An auditor most likely wouldn't allow a $2,000 detail job – she'd perhaps let you get by with a few hundred, unless you can show her some really impressive before and after photos that will sustain the expense. You need to balance the magnitude of the cost with the fact that a clean car is both ordinary and necessary for your riders' experience with you – it's necessary to maintain or improve your rating, which is vital to your business.

How much of the expense can be deducted? Only the amount that corresponds to the business percentage of the car's use. In our Hypothetical Mileage Scenario for Deductions, our imaginary driver used his car 70% for his rideshare business. If you washed your car 20 times during the year at $15 per wash, your deduction amount would be $210 – the $300 of expenses x the 70% rideshare use.

Where to deduct? Line 9 of Schedule C, "Car and truck expenses." Treat state and local sales taxes as part of the cost of car washes and detailing; do not deduct them separately on line 23 of Schedule C, "Taxes and licenses."

Casualty and Theft Losses

If your car or other items used in your rideshare business are damaged, destroyed, or stolen, you may be able to deduct part of the loss not covered by insurance. For more information, see IRS Publication 547, Casualties, Disasters, and Thefts, available online at www.irs.gov.

Where to report: Form 4684, Casualties and Thefts, and Form 4797, Sales of Business Property.

Charitable Contributions

If you're not operating as a corporation – that is, if you're running a sole proprietorship, partnership or limited liability company – then charitable contributions *from your business* aren't deductible by your business. That's not necessarily fair, of course, but the tax code is brimming with injustice.

Bear in mind that you can claim charitable contribution deductions if you itemize your deductions on Schedule A, but you can't claim deductions to offset your self-employment income.

Cleaning Materials

How much of the expense can be deducted? Like expenses for car washes, only deduct the amount that corresponds to the percentage of the car's use that was devoted to business. In our Hypothetical Mileage Scenario for Deductions, our imaginary driver used his car 70% for his rideshare business. If these materials cost you $70 over the course of the tax period, your deduction amount would be $49 – the $70 of expenses x the 70% rideshare use.

Where to deduct: Line 22 of Schedule C, "Supplies." Treat state and local sales taxes as part of the cost of car washes and detailing; do not deduct them separately on line 23 of Schedule C, "Taxes and licenses."

Clothing

Unless your rideshare company *requires* you to wear certain clothing that's to be used exclusively for work, and isn't suitable for regular streetwear, you're out of luck; don't even try it. If there *is* such a requirement by whatever company you provide service for, the expense would be taken at line 22, "Supplies."

Limo drivers can get away with a deduction for a nice suit and cap – this attire is required for such high-end professional service – but a reasonable Auditor wouldn't allow a deduction for a provider of typical rideshare service.

How much of the expenses can be deducted? If there *is* a company requirement that you purchase clothing that's to be used exclusively for work, and isn't suitable for regular "streetwear," the expenses would be deductible in their entirety.

Where to deduct: If there *is* such a requirement by the company you provide service for, the expense would be taken at line 22, "Supplies."

Credit Card and Debit Card Charges

How much of these expenses can be deducted?

If you use a credit card or debit card for business purchases, you can deduct the fees and interest – but *only* for those costs that relate to your business purchases.

You can use a personal credit or debit card for business expenses, although it's a better idea to have a card specifically for business use – see the "MANAGING YOUR RIDESHARE BUSINESS" section.

Either way, be sure to maintain good records and pro-rate business and non-business fees and interest.

If you make your credit card payments online, make sure to create pdfs of statements that contain business-related purchases. Save these to a business-specific file on your computer, and highlight the business purchases. If the item description on the statement isn't specific enough, create a contemporaneous text document explaining what the purchase was for, and the anticipated business use of the items purchased. It's unlikely that you'll be audited, but you want to be prepared, just in case.

If you have a credit or debit card that you use exclusively for your rideshare business, you can deduct all fees and interest.

Whether you use a personal card or a card dedicated strictly to business use, be *very* aware that in the event of an audit, an Auditor will be on the lookout for personal-type purchases in your statements that have been claimed as business expenses. If you've claimed personal items for business deductions, she may want to look at every purchase made on that card for the entire tax year.

Where to deduct: Deduct credit or debit card fees on Line 18 of Schedule C, "Office expense." Deduct interest charges on Line 16b of Schedule C, "Interest: Other." Treat state and local sales taxes on business purchases or services as part of the cost of the products; do not deduct them separately on line 23 of Schedule C, "Taxes and licenses."

Dash Cams

With the historically low price of dash cams now, this is probably the cheapest form of insurance you can buy. It protects you, your rideshare business, and the company you rideshare for. It can also provide evidence for (or against) you in the event of an accident, and it may even deter bad passenger behavior.

How much of this expense can be deducted?

In our Hypothetical Mileage Scenario for Deductions, our imaginary driver used his car 70% for his rideshare business. If a dash cam cost him $100, he could claim $70,

Where to deduct: Line 13 of Schedule C, "Depreciation and section 179 expense deduction," via Form 4562, "Depreciation and Amortization."

Please note that you can either depreciate a camera over a seven-year period, or expense the entire amount on your current return as a "Section 179 Deduction." Treat state and local sales taxes on business purchases or services as part of the cost of the products; do not deduct them separately on line 23 of Schedule C, "Taxes and licenses."

Depreciation of Your Rideshare Vehicle

Depreciation on your vehicle can *only* be claimed when you use the Actual Car Expenses method. *Do not claim* depreciation for your car if you're using the Standard Mileage Rate method, since depreciation is already built into the rate. See the "STANDARD MILEAGE RATE vs. ACTUAL CAR EXPENSES" section.

You're probably familiar with depreciation. The IRS defines it as "an annual income tax deduction that allows you to recover the cost or other basis of certain property over the time you use the property. It is an allowance for the wear and tear, deterioration, or obsolescence of the property."

Theoretically, it depreciation reflects the loss in value of certain items from year to year. It's a structured process of deducting the cost of a long-term business asset from your business income, a little bit at a time, over a period of years.

As mentioned previously, to be depreciable, an item must:

- Be property you own; *and,*

- Be used in your business or income-producing activity; *and,*

- Have a determinable useful life; *and,*

- Be expected to last more than one year, *and,*

- Not be excepted property.

For the purposes of this book, the item that you're most likely to want to depreciate is your car, itself, although I'll discuss other potential depreciable items, too.

You generally capitalize the cost of a motor vehicle in a business through yearly deductions for depreciation, and there are dollar limits on the amounts you can depreciate each year on passenger vehicles used in your business.

However... in a small business such as yours where you use your own car for both personal and business uses, you have a choice of methods to claim expenses for the use of your car. As I explain in the "Vehicle Expenses" section, later, there are two options available when you're deducting vehicle expenses:

- the Standard Mileage Rate, set by the IRS each year and based on the mileage used in your rideshare business, or

- the Actual Car Expenses method, in which you compute the expenses for the vehicle for the period during the year in which the car has been in business use, and pro-rate those expenses based on your rideshare mileage.

When your business use of an automobile is less than 100%, as explained before, you can only claim a deduction proportional to the business use of the item during the tax period. The same holds for property subject to depreciation – you can deduct depreciation based only on the business use.

Where to deduct: Line 13 of Schedule C, "Depreciation and section 179 expense deduction," via Form 4562, "Depreciation and Amortization."

Draw

"Draw" refers to withdrawing money from your account – either a personal account or an exclusively business account – for your personal use when you're self-employed.

Is this deductible? To paraphrase the Wizard of Oz, nobody gets to take this deduction – not nobody, no how.

Make no mistake here – as a sole proprietor, you're not an employee of your own business, and you can't pay yourself a "wage" and expect to deduct it as a business expense. This isn't to say that you can't take money out of your account to live on… it just means that you can't deduct it on your tax return.

This seems pretty obvious, but you'd be surprised how many people try to deduct personal expenses when they're self-employed, either with fraud in mind or just because they lack a basic understanding of how the tax system works.

Let's say that the taxpayer reported $20,000 of income on his Schedule C and had a number of deductions that brought his net profit down to $1,000. Under examination, the taxpayer discloses that, say, $15,000 of the deductions was money he'd drawn for his personal use – "I've got to have something to live on," he explains.

Well, of course he does, but that doesn't mean that that money wouldn't be included in his taxable income, or not reported as self-employment income. Think of it this way: If he had a salaried job, he couldn't reasonably deduct his living expenses from his taxable Form W-2 wages. But somehow the concept of self-employment leads some unfortunate folks to believe that this is allowable.

Driver's Education Courses

See Education Expenses Related to Rideshare, below.

Education Expenses Related to Rideshare

Self-employed people can deduct the costs of education related to work, but the requirements are pretty restrictive. For rideshare providers, relevant education would include Driver's Education courses and rideshare training.

To be deductible, these expenses have to be for education that either *maintains* or *improves* your job skills, or for training that your employer or a law requires "to keep your salary, status, or job," in the IRS' words.

And... even when a course of study meets either of these tests, it can only be deductible if it's *not* part of a program that would qualify you for a new trade or business, and it's *not* training that you need to meet the minimal educational requirements of your trade or business.

So, what about the cost a driver's education course? This is deductible, insomuch as it "maintains or improves your job skills." And it can be doubly valuable, insomuch as your auto insurance carrier may lower your rate based on completion of the course.

Allowable Driver's Ed expenses would include the cost of materials purchased for courses, in-person or online classroom classes, and sessions behind the wheel with a driving instructor.

Also, you might check to see if there are any programs in your state that offer a state credit or deduction for completing a driver's education course.

How about a seminar on how to improve your rideshare business? This, too would be deductible.

How much of these expenses can be deducted?

I'd suggest that the expense of a driver's ed course be pro-rated to include only the portion corresponding to your business use of the vehicle. After all, you benefit from the course whether you're using your car for business or personal use. In our Hypothetical Mileage Scenario for Deductions, our imaginary driver used his car 70% for his rideshare business. If a driver's ed

70

course cost him $50, he could deduct $35.

A seminar on improving your business would be deducted in full.

Where to deduct: Lines 27a and 48 of Schedule C, "Other expenses." Treat state and local sales taxes on business purchases or services as part of the cost of the products; do not deduct separately on line 23 of Schedule C, "Taxes and licenses."

Estimated Tax Payments

I write about the importance of making estimated tax payments in "MANAGING YOUR RIDESHARE BUSINESS," but for our purposes in this section, you need to know that estimated tax payments are *not* expenses that can be deducted from self-employment income.

However, if you've made Estimated Tax Payments for the year, you'll need to claim them in the "Payments" section of Form 1040 on line 65, "2016 estimated tax payments and amount applied from 2015 return."

Fines for Driving and Parking Offenses

You can't deduct fines or penalties that you pay to any governmental agency or instrumentality because you've violated a law, whether they were incurred while you were conducting rideshare business or not. This includes fines while the car is in motion – speeding, illegal lane changes, running red lights and the like – and parking violations.

You also can't deduct any collateral that you might've had to forfeit as a result of such violations.

First Aid Kits

How much of this expense can be deducted?

Since a first aid kit can (and presumably, *would*) be used for personal reasons as well as business reasons, the deduction should be pro-rated. In our Hypothetical Mileage Scenario for Deductions, our imaginary driver used his car 70% for his rideshare business. If a first aid kit cost him $30, he could claim $21.

71

Where to deduct: Lines 27a and 48 of Schedule C, "Other expenses." Treat state and local sales taxes on business purchases or services as part of the cost of the products; do not deduct separately on line 23 of Schedule C, "Taxes and licenses."

Floor Mats

How much of this expense can be deducted? Since floor mats will be used for personal reasons as well as business reasons, the deduction should be pro-rated. In our Hypothetical Mileage Scenario for Deductions, our imaginary driver used her car 70% for her rideshare business. If floor mats cost her $100, she could claim $70.

Where to deduct: Lines 27a and 48 of Schedule C, "Other expenses." Treat state and local sales taxes on business purchases or services as part of the cost of the products; do not deduct separately on line 23 of Schedule C, "Taxes and licenses."

Food and Drink for Passengers

Food and drink for the convenience of your passengers is partially deductible – only 50%.

Full deductions are allowed in a few circumstances, but these wouldn't appear to apply to rideshare. For example, deductible food and drink wouldn't be subject to the 50% limit if your riders reimburse you or give you some type of allowance for these expenses, and you provide adequate records of these expenses to your riders. In the IRS' terminology, if you "don't adequately account for and seek reimbursement from the client for those expenses, you are subject to ... the 50% limit."

How much of this expense can be deducted? Only half, and only for refreshments for passengers. No deduction is allowed for your own refreshments.

Where to deduct: Line 24b of Schedule C, "Deductible meals and entertainment." Treat state and local sales taxes on business purchases or services as part of the cost of the products; do not deduct these separately on line 23 of Schedule C, "Taxes and licenses."

72

Food and Drink for Yourself

Although food and drink for your passengers is at least partially deductible, you're out of luck when it comes to a deduction for your own refreshments. Just like with most other jobs, you have to eat and drink on your own dime.

Garage Rent

Garage rent is deductible whether you opt for either the Standard Mileage Rate or the Actual Car Expenses method.

How much of this expense can be deducted?

Since the garage will be used for personal and business reasons, the deduction should be pro-rated to claim only the business portion of the expense. In our Hypothetical Mileage Scenario for Deductions, our imaginary driver used his car 70% for his rideshare business. If the rent cost him $1,200 during the period that he performed rideshare service, he would claim $840 – $1,200 x his 70% business use.

Where to deduct: Line 20b of Schedule C, "Rent or lease (Other business property)." Treat state and local sales taxes on your garage rent as part of the cost of the rent; do not deduct them separately on line 23 of Schedule C, "Taxes and licenses."

Gasoline

Gasoline used for your rideshare service can only be claimed when you use the Actual Car Expenses method. *Do not claim* a deduction for it if you're using the Standard Mileage Rate method – it's already taken into account in that computation.

It's extremely important that you keep records of all of your gasoline purchases. It's a good practice to print the receipts from the pump (or inside the station, if that's not available). You may be able to show an Auditor a credit card statement showing that you paid $28.95 at Big Box Gas Company, but if the statement doesn't break down what the payment was for – it could be for beer and cigarettes, after all – then the amount could potentially be disallowed in its entirety. You don't just need to show the existence of a payment – you need

73

to be able to prove what the payment was for.

How much of this expense can be deducted? Only the amount actually used for business purposes. In our Hypothetical Mileage Scenario for Deductions, our imaginary driver used her car 70% for her rideshare business. If her gasoline expenditures at the end of the year were $2,500, she would claim $1,750 as a business deduction – $2,500 x her 70% business use of the vehicle.

Where to deduct: Line 9 of Schedule C, "Car and truck expenses." Treat state and local sales taxes on gas as part of the cost of the gas; do not deduct them separately on line 23 of Schedule C, "Taxes and licenses."

Health Insurance

You might be eligible to deduct the amount you paid for health insurance for yourself, your spouse, and your dependents – not from your business income, but from your total income on page 1 of Form 1040.

As of the time of this writing, this insurance can also cover your child who was under age 27 at the end of 2016, even if the child wasn't your dependent. For these purposes, a child includes your son, daughter, stepchild, adopted child, or foster child.

To qualify for this deduction, your business (or, all of your businesses combined, if you have more than one) must report a net profit for the year. You can't claim this as an expense if you were eligible to enroll in your or your spouse's employer's health plan.

When you're filing Schedule C or C-EZ, or F, the insurance policy can be either in your name, or in the name of the business.

How much of this expense can be deducted? To compute, see Worksheet 6A, Self Employed Health Insurance Deduction Worksheet, in IRS Publication 535, "Business Expenses." This publication is free, and is available at irs.gov.

Where to deduct: Line 29 of Form 1040, "Self-employed health insurance deduction."

Home Office Deduction

I'll only touch on this briefly, because it's highly unlikely that you'll be able to take a deduction for the business use of your home. And, just as an FYI… small businesses that claim a Home Office Deduction are audited at an exponentially greater rate than those that don't claim it, so be very wary about taking this deduction.

To qualify to claim these expenses, your use of the business part of your home must be exclusive – you have to use a specific area of your home *only* for your trade or business, and you have to use it regularly for this purpose. Even if you use a particular space for administrative tasks associated with your rideshare business, you're not likely to use it exclusively for your business.

This is not to suggest that you can't deduct office expenses associated with the business – envelopes, stamps, software, whatever – just that you probably can't take a deduction for a Home Office.

How much of this expense can be deducted? If you think you might be able to satisfy the Home Office requirements, I'll just point you to the IRS' Publication 587, Business Use of Your Home, for more information. All IRS publications are available at irs.gov.

Where to deduct, if you determine that you're eligible: Line 30 of Schedule C, "Expenses for business use of your home." You'll also need to complete and attach Form 8829, "Expenses for Business Use of Your Home," if you're not using the "simplified method" on line 30. Again, though – be very careful about claiming this.

Incorporation Fees

How much of this expense can be deducted? If you've chosen to incorporate your rideshare business, the entire amount is deductible.

Where to deduct: If you paid a professional to incorporate your business, claim the deduction on line 17, "Legal and professional services." If you did it yourself, take the deduction on line 23, "Taxes and licenses."

IRA Contributions

IRA Contributions aren't deductible as a business expense, but can be deducted on line 32 of Form 1040, "IRA deduction." This deduction can't be taken if your income is above a certain threshold, and there is a maximum amount that you can claim. For additional information, see the Instructions for Form 1040, available at irs.gov.

Interest Expenses

Interest on a personal loan – for example, on your car – is deductible as a business expense, but only to the extent that it relates to the business use. These expenses are deductible whether you use the Standard Mileage Rate or the Actual Car Expenses method.

Interest on other items can also be deducted. The largest typical expense, barring significant repairs to your auto, is probably gasoline. You'll need to pro-rate the interest paid on gasoline in the same way that the gasoline itself was pro-rated – that is, if the business use of the vehicle was 70% for the year, you'd have to figure 70% of the interest paid on that gasoline. This goes for all other business items you purchase, as well.

How much of these expenses can be deducted?

In our hypothetical example, we determined that 70% of the miles put on your car for the year were for business purposes. If the interest on your car loan was $500 for the year, then $350 would be deductible.

A similar calculation would need to be performed on other business expenses that you deduct. There may be a point at which you don't even bother with the calculation, because the cost of an item is relatively small. That's fine. Remember the "Rule of Seven" – for every $7 you can lower your self-employment income, you save $1 in self-employment tax. If you find yourself calculating pennies of interest on the purchase of an item, just bear in mind that you've got to save 700 pennies in deductions just to achieve that $1 in savings, and it may not be worth your time.

Where to deduct: Line 16b of Schedule C, "Interest (Other)."

76

Standard Mileage Rate

If you're using the Standard Mileage Rate to deduct your vehicle's expenses for the year, you can't claim any portion of your lease payment as an additional deduction, since the lease expense is considered to be included in the Standard Mileage Rate.

Actual Car Expenses

If you're using the Actual Car Expenses method, on the other hand, you can deduct the portion of your lease expenses that are attributable to the business use of the vehicle. So, if your lease payment for the year was $3,000, and the business use of the vehicle was 70% as in our hypothetical, your lease deduction would be $2,100.

BEWARE, though – there are a couple of twists.

Advance Lease Payments

If you were required to make an advance lease payment, you have to spread this out over the entire lease period.

> *Example.* On January 1st, Reymundo leased a car that he's using for his rideshare business. As part of the lease agreement, he had to make an initial payment of $800. He leased the car for four years. Assuming our hypothetical scenario in which he used the car for business purposes 70% of the time, his yearly deduction for the advance lease payment would be $140 – $800 ÷ 4 year = $200 per year; $200 x his 70% business use = $140. Note that if Reymundo leased this car on July 1st, he'd only be able to deduct $70 for that first year – half of the $140 – since he leased the car for only half of that year.

Inclusion Amounts

When you lease a car for more than 30 days, the amount you can deduct will probably be limited, albeit slightly.

Your deduction will be limited if the car you use for rideshare is a "luxury" car. You're probably thinking that your car wouldn't be classified as a luxury car, but for these purposes, this is how your car will be defined when its fair market value is $19,000 or more. Luxury isn't what it used to be.

The amount by which you'll need to reduce your lease deduction (referred to as an "inclusion amount") is based on the fair market value of your vehicle – as of the first day of the lease term.

The inclusion amounts are published each year in IRS Publication 463, "Travel, Entertainment, Gift, and Car Expenses." There's a good explanation of inclusion amounts in the "Leasing a Car" section, and the inclusion amounts for car are in Appendices A-1 through A-5 in that publication.

However, I'll walk you through an example.

Example: Inga has leased a car for four years at $3,600 per year, beginning January 1st, 2016.

Using the 70% business usage of the car from our generic hypothetical, her deduction for a year would be $2,520 – that's the $3,600 annual lease payment x her 70% business usage.

The car had a $25,000 fair market value on the first day of the lease. If you'll look at Appendix A-5 in Publication 463 for 2016 tax returns, you'll see that it contains the inclusion amounts for cars first leased in 2016. The inclusion amount for a car with a $25,000 fair market value, in the first year of its lease, was $16. Since Inga's business use of the car was 70%, her inclusion amount will be $11.20.

Therefore, her lease deduction for the year is $2,508.80 – her basic $2,520 lease deduction, *minus* the $11.20 inclusion amount. (And yes, you're right... calling it an "inclusion" amount is very misleading.)

Where to deduct: Line 9 of Schedule C, "Car and truck expenses."

Maintenance of and Repairs to Your Vehicle

Repairs for the car you use for your rideshare service can only be claimed when you use the Actual Car Expenses method. *Do not claim* if you're using the Standard Mileage Rate method – it's already taken into account in that calculation.

And, this is probably obvious… you can't deduct expenses that have been paid by your insurance company, just what's been paid out of your own pocket.

If you incur large repair bills during the year, be sure to run your deduction calculation using both the Actual Car Expenses method and the Standard Mileage Rate method.

How much of these expenses can be deducted? As with other vehicle expenses, you can only deduct the portion attributable to your business use of the vehicle. So, if your repairs for the year amounted to $1,200, and the business use of the vehicle was 70% as in our basic hypothetical, your deduction would be $840.

Where to deduct: You really have the option of reporting these expenses on either line 9 of Schedule C, "Car and truck expenses," or line 21, "Repairs and maintenance." Line 21 is the more logical spot, but claiming the repairs and maintenance would be consistent with where they're reported as part of the Standard Mileage Rate. Remember to treat state and local sales taxes as part of the cost of maintenance and repairs; do not deduct these taxes separately on line 23 of Schedule C, "Taxes and licenses."

Memberships

If you're a member of an organization that's related to the business aspects of your rideshare activity (as opposed to an organization, for example, that's strictly social in nature), you can deduct the expense of membership.

How much of these expenses can be deducted? You can deduct these expenses to the extent that they apply to your rideshare business.

Where to deduct: Line 27a of Schedule C, "Other expenses." Also include a description and the amount of the expense in Part V of Schedule C. If you

79

need to list more than nine items in Part V and you're filing a paper return, include the first eight items in Part V, and indicate "See attachment" on the last line. Then, attach an additional document listing the remaining deductions. (If you're using tax software, additional lines should be able to populate, or the software will automatically create and title an appropriate attachment.)

Mileage Trackers

There are some free apps are out there that can track your mileage, but if you pay for one, it's deductible.

How much of these expenses can be deducted? This expense should be deducted in full, since the only reason for having it is tracking miles for your business. You don't need to restrict the deduction to a percentage based on your business mileage percentage.

Where to deduct: Line 27a of Schedule C, "Other expenses." Also include a description and the amount of the expense in Part V of Schedule C. If you need to list more than nine items in Part V and you're filing a paper return, include the first eight items in Part V, and indicate "See attachment" on the last line. Then, attach an additional document listing the remaining deductions. (If you're using tax software, additional lines should be able to populate, or the software will automatically create and title an appropriate attachment.)

Miscellaneous Expenses

I don't doubt that there might be some reasonable rideshare expenses that I haven't gone into further detail about. Items like, say, USB chargers, mobile routers, electronic toll transponders... just use your imagination.

Just remember this... if an expense is for something that's among the items included in the Standard Mileage Rate, *and* if you're using the Standard Mileage Rate for the tax period, then the item can't be deducted.

Outside of that... if the item is "ordinary and reasonable" for the rideshare business, then it should be deductible. I'd suggest reading the earlier sections, "A Deduction Must Be "Ordinary" and "Necessary,"" and "Ward Cleaver and the Concept of Reasonableness," and consider realistically whether the item has a reasonable use for rideshare.

How much of these expenses can be deducted?

If the item has a business and personal use, only the portion that's relevant to your business. In our hypothetical example, we determined that 70% of the miles put on our driver's car for the year were for business purposes. If her expense for a given item was $10, then $70 would be deductible.

If the item was used exclusively for business – and, be reasonable here – then it can be deducted in its entirety.

If an item is likely to wear out within a year of purchase, it may be deducted in its entirety. If it has a longer expected useful life span, it can be either depreciated over a period of years, or taken as a Section 179 Deduction.

Where to deduct:

Items with an expected useful life of over one year should be either depreciated over a period of years, or taken as Section 179 deductions, in which case you can most likely claim the entire amount of the expense on one tax return. Either way, you'd take this deduction on Line 13 of Schedule C, "Depreciation and section 179 expense deduction," via Form 4562, "Depreciation and Amortization." To determine the depreciation period of an item, see IRS Publication 946, "How To Depreciate Property."

If you can't easily determine which line on Schedule C applies to an expense, just claim short-lifespan items on Line 27a of Schedule C, "Other expenses (from line 48)." When you enter an amount on line 27a, make sure that you've included the items relevant to the expense in Part V of Schedule C.

It's a *really* bad idea to just list something in Part V of Schedule C ("Other Expenses") simply as "Miscellaneous" or "Other," particularly if the amount is fairly large relative to either your business income or other business deductions. This raises a red flag for an auditor, so try to describe all the items in Part V with some specificity.

You'll note that Part V has only nine lines. If you need to list more than nine items in Part V and you're filing a paper return, include the first eight items in Part V, and indicate "See attachment" on the last line. Then, attach an additional document listing the remaining deductions. (If you're using tax software, additional lines will be able to populate, or the software will automatically create and title an appropriate attachment.)

Treat state and local sales taxes on these expenses as part of their costs; do not deduct the taxes separately on line 23 of Schedule C, "Taxes and licenses."

Motor Oil and Oil Changes

Like gasoline, motor oil and oil changes can only be claimed when you use the Actual Car Expenses method. *Do not claim* if you're using the Standard Mileage Rate method – the expense is already taken into account in that computation.

How much of this expense can be deducted? The full expense amount, pro-rated to your business usage of the car. In our Hypothetical Mileage Scenario for Deductions, our imaginary driver used her car 70% for her rideshare business. If her oil and oil change costs at the end of the year were $150, she would claim $105 as a business deduction – $150 x her 70% business use of the vehicle.

Where to deduct: Line 9 of Schedule C, "Car and truck expenses." Treat state and local sales taxes as part of the cost of the oil; do not deduct them separately on line 23 of Schedule C, "Taxes and licenses."

Music System

The music system that was in your car when you purchased it can't be deducted separately – it's already being accounted for in your car's depreciation, if you're using the Actual Car Expenses method, or in the Standard Mileage Rate, if you're using that option.

However, if you install a new system, or upgrade your current system, a portion of that expense can be deducted.

I'll also point out that an Auditor most likely won't allow a complete deduction – even limited to business usage – if you've tricked out your car with, say, a $5,000 sound system. Remember the standards for taking business deductions – "Ordinary and Necessary." Don't foolishly buy a high-priced sound system simply for your own benefit, and try to have the American taxpayer subsidize it through your deduction. Don't go crazy.

82

How much of this expense can be deducted? As with other vehicle expenses, you can only deduct the portion attributable to your business use of the vehicle. So, if an upgraded system costs $800, and the business use of the vehicle was 70% as in our basic hypothetical, your deduction – or your depreciable amount, whichever you choose – would be $560.

Where to deduct: Line 13 of Schedule C, "Depreciation and section 179 expense deduction."

Please note that you can either depreciate this over a five-year period, or expense the entire amount on your current return as a "Section 179 Deduction."

You'll also need to complete and attach Form 4562, "Depreciation and Amortization."

Treat state and local sales taxes on business purchases as part of the cost of the products; do not deduct them separately on line 23 of Schedule C, "Taxes and licenses."

Navigation Apps

How much of this expense can be deducted? I suggested earlier that you can deduct the expense of a mileage tracker in full, because its sole purpose is for your business. Not so with a navigation app, since it has both a business and personal use. You can only deduct the portion attributable to your business use of the vehicle. So, if an app costs you $25, and the business use of the vehicle was 70% as in our basic hypothetical, your deduction would be $17.50.

Where to deduct: Line 27a of Schedule C, "Other expenses." Treat state and local sales taxes on business purchases as part of the cost of the products; do not deduct them separately on line 23 of Schedule C, "Taxes and licenses."

Office Supplies

Unlike the Home Office deduction, which probably isn't viable for rideshare drivers, office supplies can be readily deducted – to the extent that they're used for your business.

However, I should point out that, because you're providing rideshare services, a large deduction for office expenses will probably be a red flag for an Auditor. He'd probably have a difficult time envisioning significant office expenses, considering the nature of your work.

How much of these expenses can be deducted? Only the portion attributable to your business. This can be hard to track, since it's very easy to co-mingle office-type items that can be used for both personal and business use. Because of this, it might be a good idea to buy "dedicated" items – for example, a printer cartridge or a package of printing paper that you devote *only* to business use.

Where to deduct: Line 18 of Schedule C, "Office expense." Treat state and local sales taxes on business purchases or services as part of the cost of the products; do not deduct separately on line 23 of Schedule C, "Taxes and licenses."

Parking Fees

How much of these expenses can be deducted? If a parking fee is paid while in the course of business, deduct it in its entirety.

Where to deduct: Line 9 of Schedule C, "Car and truck expenses."

Personal Property Tax

These expenses are deductible whether you use the Standard Mileage Rate or the Actual Car Expenses method.

You have a couple of choices here for state or local personal property taxes on a car you used in your rideshare business.

If you're itemizing deductions on Schedule A (Itemized Deductions,) your first option is to write the entire amount off there, on line 7, "Personal property taxes."

More likely than not, however, the better idea is to deduct the *business* portion of state and local personal property taxes on a car used in your business on line 23 of Schedule C, "Taxes and licenses."

How much of these expenses can be deducted? Only the portion attributable to your business. In our hypothetical example, 70% of the miles our driver put on her car for the year were for business purposes. If your property tax on the car was $300 for the year, then $210 would be deductible as a business expense.

But if you itemize deductions using Schedule A, you can include the remainder of the taxes – that would be $90 – on line 7 of Schedule A.

Why would you even bother separate the amounts like this? First of all, you need to segregate your business expenses from your personal expenses. But, from a dollars-and-cents standpoint, you lower your net self-employment income and therefore your self-employment tax when you claim the business portion of the tax on Schedule C.

Where to deduct: Line 23 of Schedule C, "Taxes and licenses," and, as appropriate, line 7 of Schedule A, "Personal property taxes."

Phones and Accessories

Deductible expenses include cell phones, Bluetooth, phone mounts, wireless plans, chargers and cables.

Any cell-phone type costs that are related to ridesharing business, and which are paid by you, are deductible. Any such services or products that are provided to you by your rideshare company, for which you pay nothing, may not be deducted. (I know, it seems like common sense, but you'd be surprised how many people will try to deduct items that are paid for by someone else.)

How much of these expenses can be deducted? You can only deduct the amounts that actually correspond to your rideshare business, and the percentage of your car's use that was devoted to business isn't really relevant. Bear in mind, however, that if an auditor sees a $1,200 cell phone expense and you've only earned $3,000 with your rideshare business, a red flag is going to go up.

85

Where to deduct: Line 27a of Schedule C, "Other expenses (from line 48)."

Also, be sure to include a description of the item and its expense amount in Part V of Schedule C. If you need to list more than nine items in Part V and you're filing a paper return, include the first eight items in Part V, and indicate "See attachment" on the last line. Then, attach an additional document listing the remaining deductions. (If you're using tax software, additional lines will be able to populate, or the software will automatically create and title an appropriate attachment.)

Treat state and local sales taxes on business purchases or services as part of the cost of the products; do not deduct separately on line 23 of Schedule C, "Taxes and licenses."

Retirement Contributions

SEP, SIMPLE, and qualified plans can provide you with a tax-favored way to save for retirement. When you're a sole proprietor, you can deduct contributions you make to a plan for yourself. Earnings on the contributions are generally tax free until you receive distributions from the plan.

There are a multitude of factors that you need to consider when you're self-employed and are setting up a retirement plan, and that's outside the subject matter of this book. However, IRS Publication 560, "Retirement Plans for Small Business," is a wonderful resource, and is available for download at irs.gov. This pub explains the basic features of SEP, SIMPLE, and qualified plans. It'll also provide you with information about what type of plans you can set up, how to set a plan up, how much you can contribute to a plan, and how much of the contribution is deductible.

I've also included a brief section on the Retirement Savings Contributions Credit near the end of the book. This is worth looking at if you'd like the federal government to help subsidize your retirement savings via a tax credit.

Where to deduct: Line 28 of Form 1040, Self-employed SEP, SIMPLE, and qualified plans.

Rideshare Insurance

Generally, car insurance can only be claimed when using the Actual Car Expenses method. A policyholder would not be able to claim it if she was using the Standard Mileage Rate method – it's already factored in to the calculation.

Luckily, insurance provided by rideshare companies (above and beyond what you normally pay for car insurance) is paid for by the company, so you can't deduct it on your return.

However, these insurance policies will generally only cover you when you're en route to pick up a passenger, or when you're actually transporting the fare. That means that you're not covered if you're logged on to the Driver App and just waiting for customers. (Check the Terms of Agreement of your rideshare service to see what conditions apply to you.) In other words, during this period of time, however brief, you won't have collision coverage from your rideshare company, and your personal insurer most likely isn't going to cover you, either. In fact, your insurance company can actually even drop your coverage, altogether, if they discover that you're using your car for ridesharing purposes.

If the insurance provided by your rideshare company doesn't cover damages in this instance, it's worthwhile to consider purchasing what's simply known as "rideshare insurance."

A lot of drivers don't carry this gap insurance, but it's worth considering. According to a recent survey by the Rideshare Guy, about 80% of drivers don't have this insurance. (The wonderful Rideshare Guy website is well worth checking out.)

Can this expense be deducted when I claim the Standard Mileage Rate?
Logically it should be deductible, even when you choose the Standard Mileage Rate, since this type of insurance would be purchased *in addition to* your normal car insurance, and strictly for business purposes. However, logic doesn't always rule the day when it comes to tax law. Typically, as I've noted previously, auto insurance is deemed to be included in the Standard Mileage Rate. Under the rules currently in place, gap insurance does not appear to be deductible when claiming the Standard Mileage Rate. Claim it at your own peril.

Can this expense be deducted when I claim Actual Car Expenses? Yes. It is both ordinary and necessary.

How much of the expense can be deducted? Generally, a deduction for vehicle insurance would be pro-rated based only on the business use of your vehicle. However, the best thinking is that, because this so-called "gap insurance" applies specifically and solely to the business use of your vehicle, no pro-ration is necessary – it can be written off in its entirety.

Where to deduct: Include it on line 15 of Schedule C, "Insurance." It could alternatively be reported on line 9 of Schedule C, "Car and truck expenses," since this would be consistent with where insurance is reported when it's included in the Standard Mileage Rate.

Satellite Radio Subscription

This expense would be deductible since it can increase your passengers' enjoyment of the service you're providing, therefore potentially resulting in higher ratings, and potentially more work for you.

How much of the expense can be deducted? You'll need to pro-rate the expense in accordance with your business miles. In our hypothetical example, 70% of the miles our driver put on her car for the year were for business purposes. If these expenses were $240 for the year, then $168 would be deductible as a business expense.

Where to deduct: Include it on line 27a, "Other expenses."

Seat Cushions, Seat Covers and Other Items for Comfort

Here, I'm referencing not only your riders' comfort, but your own, as well.

If, for example, you suffer from back pain, and special cushions or other comfort items helps prevent pain while you're ridesharing, then it would be deductible, to the extent of its business use.

Likewise, if you purchase comfort items to be used by your passengers, these would also be deductible. The question of how much is deductible is trickier. To claim the entirety of these expenses, the items would need to be exclusively for the use of rideshare passengers, as opposed to other riders – friends, family, etc. If these aren't used by people other than rideshare passengers, claim the entire expense. Otherwise, it's safer to restrict your deduction to the pro-rated business use amount.

How much of the expense can be deducted? Let's assume that these comfort items cost $100. Using the rate from our hypothetical scenario in which 70% of the mileage you put on your car during the year is attributable to your rideshare services, the deductible amount will be $70.

Where to deduct: Line 27a of Schedule C, "Other expenses." Also include a description and the amount of the expense in Part V of Schedule C. Treat state and local sales taxes on business purchases or services as part of the cost of the products; do not deduct separately on line 23 of Schedule C, "Taxes and licenses."

Self-Employment Tax (Social Security and Medicare Taxes)

Federal social insurance taxes are imposed on employers and their employees, generally made up of a 12.4% tax on wages up to an annual wage maximum for Social Security, and a tax of 2.9% of all wages for Medicare.

When you earn wages, half of each of these amounts is paid by your employer, and the other half is paid by you through payroll deductions.

But when you're self-employed, the entire amounts are paid by you since you are, in essence, both the employer and the employee. This is where the "Rule of Seven" I mentioned earlier comes in – you're paying self-employment tax on 15.3% x .9235 of your self-employment income, roughly one-seventh of your net earnings.

You pay these taxes on your self-employment income via Schedule SE, Self-Employment Tax. Your deduction for paying these taxes is one-half of the SE Tax you pay. You can't deduct the one-half SE tax deduction as a business expense on Schedule C; rather, you claim it on Form 1040.

Where to deduct: Line 27 of Form 1040.

Seminars and Other Training

See Education Expenses.

Signs for Your Car

These are deductible in full, since they're only used for business purposes. Such signs can come in extremely handy, helping your passenger easily identify your car when you've come for pick-up, saving time for you both. They're especially helpful in crowded pick-up areas, or when you're picking up from a hotel or restaurant where some pesky employee might otherwise be inclined to shoo you away.

How much of the expense can be deducted? This expense can be deducted in full.

Where to deduct: Line 27a of Schedule C, "Other expenses." Also include a description and the amount of the expense in Part V of Schedule C. Treat state and local sales taxes on business purchases or services as part of the cost of the products; do not deduct separately on line 23 of Schedule C, "Taxes and licenses."

Software – GPS and Other

Software is generally depreciated over three years, but sometimes software has a short life span and can be expensed in its entirety in one year.

One example of this "short life span" software is the update for your Global Positioning System. These updates can come out multiple times a year, and can therefore be expensed in the year they were bought.

You can now also claim a "Section 179 Deduction" for off-the shelf software, which allows you to claim a one-time expense for the entire purchase price, as opposed to depreciating it over the three year period.

How much of these expenses can be deducted? Only the portion attributable to your business. Depending on the item, it could be 100% business use, but in most cases, you'll probably need to pro-rate using your percentage of business miles. Be reasonable in your assessment.

90

Where to deduct: Line 13 of Schedule C, "Depreciation and section 179 expense deduction," via Form 4562, "Depreciation and Amortization." Please note that you can generally either depreciate software over a three-year period, or expense the entire amount on your current return as a "Section 179 Deduction." But, either way, only calculate this based on your business use of the item.

For software and updates that need to be purchased at least once a year, claim this on Line 27a of Schedule C, "Other expenses." Also include a description and the amount of the expense in Part V of Schedule C. Treat state and local sales taxes on business purchases or services as part of the cost of the products; do not deduct separately on line 23 of Schedule C, "Taxes and licenses."

Software – Tax Return Preparation

As noted earlier, software is generally depreciated over three years, but software with a short life span – i.e., a program that, by necessity, must be updated often – can be expensed in its entirety in one year.

How much of these expenses can be deducted?

You can only deduct tax prep software to the extent that it's actually used for your business purposes, but this amount is generally pretty easy to ascertain.

Say that I&S Black has a regular individual income tax program that retails for $49.95, a version that you'd probably use if you didn't have self-employment income. But it also has a "Self-Employed" software package that you buy for $99.95. The amount that you can deduct is the difference – $50.00.

You'll also be able to claim the remainder – the software for the non-business portion of your income tax return preparation – on Schedule A as an Itemized Deduction.

Where to deduct:

You can deduct the business-related part of your tax preparation expenses – in the example above, it's $50.00 – on line 17 of Schedule C, "Legal and professional services."

You can deduct the non-business-related portion – $49.95, in the above scenario – on line 22 of Schedule A, "Tax preparation fees."

Treat state and local sales taxes as part of the cost of the software; do not deduct these taxes separately on line 23 of Schedule C, "Taxes and licenses."

Standard Mileage Allowance

See STANDARD MILEAGE RATE vs. ACTUAL CAR EXPENSES.

Startup Costs

Startup costs include any amounts paid or incurred in connection with creating an active trade or business, or investigating the creation or acquisition of an active trade or business.

These costs are generally considered capital expenditures, meaning you'd have to amortize them over a period of years – a process similar to depreciation. However, you can elect to deduct up to $5,000 of business startup and $5,000 of organizational costs paid or incurred after October 22, 2004. The $5,000 deduction is reduced by the amount your total startup or organizational costs exceed $50,000. So, for example if your startup costs are $52,000, the maximum amount you can claim in the current year is $3,000 -- $5,000 minus ($52,000 minus $50,000). This doesn't seem like a likely scenario for your rideshare business. Any remaining costs must be amortized over a 15-year period.

How much of these expenses can be deducted? Only the portion attributable to your business.

Where to deduct: Line 27a of Schedule C, "Other expenses." Also include a description and the amount of the expense in Part V of Schedule C. Treat state and local sales taxes on business purchases or services as part of the cost of the products; do not deduct separately on line 23 of Schedule C, "Taxes and licenses."

92

Most of these items probably won't apply to you as a rideshare driver, but I'll pass them all on in the interests of completeness, and just in case they're relevant to you.

Deductible Amounts

- State and local sales taxes that are imposed on you, as the *provider* of services. If you collected this tax from your rideshare passenger, you have to include the amount collected in gross receipts or sales on line 1, "Gross receipts or sales." These taxes are effectively "zeroed out," as far as your business is concerned; you're merely a pass-through entity for the taxes.
- Real estate and personal property taxes you pay that relate to your business assets.
- Licenses and regulatory fees your business incurs, paid every year to state or local governments.
- Social Security and Medicare taxes paid to match the required withholding from your employees' wages. You should reduce your deduction by the amount shown on line 4 of Form 8846, Credit for Employer Social Security and Medicare Taxes Paid on Certain Employee Tips.
- Federal unemployment tax that your business paid.
- Federal highway use tax.
- Contributions you made to state unemployment insurance funds or disability benefit funds, but only if they're deemed to be taxes under the laws of your jurisdiction.

Non-Deductible Amounts

- State and local sales taxes that you paid on property purchased for use in your business. You may notice that I've pointed this out in various places in the text; this is for those readers who might just skip around within the book to subjects they're concerned about. Treat these taxes as part of the cost of the property itself, and report on the line relevant to that property, rather than deducting the taxes separately on line 23 of Schedule C, "Taxes and licenses."

- Federal income taxes, including your self-employment tax. You will, however, be able to deduct half of your self-employment tax on Form 1040, line 27 (or Form 1040NR, line 27, when covered under the U.S. social security system due to an international social security agreement).
- Estate and gift taxes.
- Taxes assessed to pay for improvements, such as paving and sewers.
- Taxes on your home or personal use property.
- State and local sales taxes imposed on the *buyer* of your service, that you were required to collect and pay over to state or local governments. These taxes aren't included in gross receipts or sales nor are they a deductible expense. However, if the state or local government allowed you to retain any part of the sales tax you collected, you need to include that amount as income on line 6 of Schedule C, 'Other income, including federal and state gasoline or fuel tax credit or refund."
- Other taxes and license fees not related to your business.

These expenses are not built into the Standard Mileage Rate, so they can be claimed whether you use the Standard Mileage Rate or the Actual Car Expenses method.

How much of these expenses can be deducted? Only the portion attributable to your business.

Where to deduct: Line 23 of Schedule C, "Taxes and licenses."

Timers

Timers are useful items when waiting… and waiting… and waiting for passengers to show up at the agreed location. The rideshare corporation you contract for may have a specific time period that you're required to wait before abandoning the job, and you may even earn a cancellation fee when the passenger doesn't show.

How much of the expense can be deducted? Timers can be very cheap, so

94

be reasonable as to the amount you spend. The entire amount can be deducted, since this has a use that's strictly for your business.

Where to deduct: Line 27a of Schedule C, "Other expenses (from line 48)." Also include a description and the amount of the expense in Part V of Schedule C. Treat state and local sales taxes as part of the cost of the timer; don't deduct these taxes separately on line 23 of Schedule C, "Taxes and licenses."

This Book

How much of these expenses can be deducted? Yes, even this book is deductible. In its entirety, since it's only useful for business purposes.

Where to deduct: Line 18 of Schedule C, "Office expense." Treat state and local sales taxes on business purchases or services as part of the cost of the products; do not deduct separately on line 23 of Schedule C, "Taxes and licenses."

Tip Boxes

Although tipping was initially forbidden by some rideshare companies, it's now widely permitted and considered a normal event. Be aware that tips must be included in your rideshare income.

As I mentioned in the Income portion of this book, cash tips need to be included in your self-employment income, just as tips charged to cards are. You should maintain a log of cash tips received.

How much of these expenses can be deducted? If you've put up a sign or made a tip box available in your vehicle, the costs associated with these can be deducted in their entirety.

Where to deduct: Line 27a of Schedule C, "Other expenses (from line 48)." Also include a description and the amount of the expense in Part V of Schedule C. Treat state and local sales taxes as part of the costs; do not deduct these taxes separately on line 23 of Schedule C, "Taxes and licenses."

Tires and Wheels

Tires and wheels for the car you use for your rideshare service can only be claimed when you use the Actual Car Expenses method. *Do not claim* if you're using the Standard Mileage Rate method, as these expenses are already taken into account in that rate.

I'll also point out that an Auditor most likely won't allow a complete deduction – even when limited to business usage – if you've tricked out your car with high-dollar wheels. Remember the standards for taking business deductions – "Ordinary and Necessary." Don't buy a luxury-type item and try to have your fellow taxpayers subsidize it.

How much of the expenses can be deducted? Again – you can only claim these expenses if you're using the Actual Car Expenses method, and you can only deduct a pro-rated proportion of the costs based on your business mileage during the tax period. In our hypothetical scenario, 70% of the miles our driver put on her car during the year were for business purposes. If new wheels or tires cost her $700, she can deduct $490.

Where to deduct: Line 9 of Schedule C, "Car and truck expenses." Treat state and local sales taxes on business purchases or services as part of the cost of the products; do not deduct separately on line 23 of Schedule C, "Taxes and licenses."

Tolls

How much of the expenses can be deducted? Tolls are fully deductible when they're paid for your ridesharing business, whether you use the Standard Mileage Rate method or the Actual Car Expenses option.

Where to deduct: Line 9 of Schedule C, "Car and truck expenses."

Tools and Car Safety Items

The expenses of items like an auto tool kit, jumper cables, a battery jump pack, a tire pressure gauge and inflator, a spare tire and a tire flat repair kit are "ordinary" and "necessary," in IRS parlance.

You can deduct the expense of tools if they're likely to wear out within a year of purchase. Tools with a longer expected useful life can be either depreciated over a period of years, or taken as a Section 179 Deduction.

How much of the expenses can be deducted? Since these items will benefit you whether you're transporting passengers or not, you should only deduct a pro-rated proportion of the costs based on your business mileage during the tax period.

Where to deduct:

For items likely to wear out within a year of purchase, claim your expenses on Line 22 of Schedule C, "Supplies."

Mechanic-type tools should be either depreciated over a five-year period, or taken as a Section 179 deduction, in which you'd claim the entire expense on one tax return. Either way, you'd take this deduction on Line 13 of Schedule C, "Depreciation and section 179 expense deduction," via Form 4562, "Depreciation and Amortization."

Towels and Other Items for Clean-Up

As with car washes, these expenses are deductible. Maintaining a clean car is essential to your rideshare business – and to your rideshare ratings.

How much of the expenses can be deducted?

A deduction should be taken in proportion to your business use of the car during the tax period. In our hypothetical scenario, 70% of the miles our driver put on his car during the year were for business purposes. If these items cost him $60, he can deduct $42.

Where to deduct: Line 22 of Schedule C, "Supplies." Treat state and local sales taxes as part of the cost; do not deduct these taxes separately on line 23 of Schedule C, "Taxes and licenses."

97

Vehicle Registration Fees

This expense is only deductible if you use the Actual Car Expenses method. Registration fees are considered to be included in the Standard Mileage Rate, so you can't claim the expense when you use that option.

How much of the expenses can be deducted? If you use the Actual Car Expenses method, you can deduct a pro-rated proportion of the fees based on your business mileage. In our hypothetical example, 70% of the miles our driver put on her car during the year were for business purposes. If your registration fees amounted to $50, you can deduct $35.

Where to deduct: Line 23 of Schedule C, "Taxes and licenses."

Vomit Bags

Hey, it happens. After all, rideshare is a godsend to people who would formerly drink and drive.

How much of the expense can be deducted?

You're fine in deducting the expense in its entirety, as long as the items are used exclusively for rideshare purposes.

If used for personal, as well as business, purposes, take a deduction in proportion to your business use of the car during the tax period. In our hypothetical scenario, 70% of the miles our driver put on her car during the year were for business purposes. If these items cost her $20, she can deduct $14.

Where to deduct: Line 22 of Schedule C, "Supplies." Treat state and local sales taxes as part of the cost; do not deduct these taxes separately on line 23 of Schedule C, "Taxes and licenses."

Weapons for Self-Protection

I wouldn't suggest that you take a deduction for any weapons you might carry for self-protection while providing your rideshare service.

This is based on two main thoughts – number one, that it's almost surely not deductible and, secondly, that the tax benefit you'd gain would be relatively

98

small, anyway. Considering these two notions together, it's not worth risking the deduction and a potential audit.

Deductions for weapons of various kinds are widely allowed in a number of professions. Think of security guards – the ownership of a handgun for a guard is not only "ordinary and necessary," in Internal Revenue Code parlance, but it's also probably a requirement for the vast majority of companies that employ them.

The main reason that rideshare drivers might want to carry a weapon is pretty obvious – self-protection. There've been a number of assaults on drivers. And you're probably only too aware that you, as a driver, will at some point or another have to deal with strangers who may be drunk, high or otherwise not in a pristine state of mind.

The rideshare companies want drivers and their passengers to be safe, certainly, but they're also very concerned about the company's potential liability in a possible scenario in which a driver might attack passengers or others. This fear became a reality last year a rideshare driver in Michigan is alleged to have driven around Kalamazoo, shooting and killing people in various spots around town, all the while picking up and dropping off passengers between the shootings. Luckily no passengers were harmed, but that's small consolation to the families who lost their loved ones.

In fact, at least two of the two major rideshare providers have official policies prohibiting weapons, which you should be aware of.

Uber's website has stated: "Our goal is to ensure that everyone has a safe and reliable ride. That's why Uber prohibits riders and drivers from carrying firearms of any kind in a vehicle while using our app. Anyone who violates this policy may lose access to Uber."

Lyft goes even further: "With respect to your use of the Lyft Platform and your participation in the Services, you agree that you will not…. carry any weapons." Like Uber, Lyft may terminate its agreement with a driver upon breach of this clause.

Clearly, Lyft doesn't prohibit just firearms, as Uber does – it bans "any weapons," however that may be defined.

It's not my intention here to take a position on whether or not these policies are valid or not, although I can understand your concerns as a driver. The importance of these policies, from an income tax standpoint, goes to whether or not a deduction for a weapon of some sort is "ordinary and necessary."

A weapon will typically be deductible for business purposes if you can demonstrate that it's needed for safety, if it's legally obtained, if it's legal to have with you while on duty, and (*wait for it...*) the company that you're driving for permits you to carry the weapon.

At this point in time, Uber and Lyft are the leaders in the rideshare industry, and their policies carry a lot of weight. Their official positions give very heavy weight to the proposition that carrying a weapon while driving is neither ordinary nor reasonable.

Let's go back to our definitions. An expense is ordinary if it's common and accepted in your field of business. The expense is necessary if it's helpful and appropriate for the business.

The driver could legitimately argue that a weapon is helpful and appropriate for rideshare drivers – therefore meeting the "necessary" test.

But is the expense of a weapon ordinary – that is, is it common and accepted in the industry?

The answer has to be no. It's very hard to determine how many rideshare drivers carry weapons... but we *do* know that industry leaders *explicitly* forbid the carrying of weapons by their drivers while on the job.

It may well be the case that you actually know other drivers who've written off a weapon of some sort on their tax returns, and haven't received any adverse notifications from the IRS. Do not mistake this as some sort of tacit acceptance of this deduction by the IRS. This simply means that these deductions weren't caught and disallowed. The IRS accepts roughly 150 million individual income tax returns each year. Things slip through, and that's just a fact of life.

These are very valuable apps to have, unless maybe you're in the sunny climes of SoCal, where the weather is almost always nice.

When an app alerts you of imminent bad weather – periods during which people might not want to drive, themselves – you can plan your time to perhaps take advantage of more fares and possible surge pricing.

How much of the expense can be deducted? An Auditor would most likely limit this expense based on business use. It has both business and personal purposes, so you can only deduct the portion attributable to your business use of the vehicle. If this item cost our driver $30, and the business use of the vehicle was 70% as in our basic hypothetical, her deduction would be $21.

Where to deduct: Line 27a of Schedule C, "Other expenses." Treat state and local sales taxes on business purchases as part of the cost of the products; do not deduct them separately on line 23 of Schedule C, "Taxes and licenses."

101

TIPS FOR PREPARING YOUR SCHEDULE C

Line A, Principal business or profession, including product or service. Simply enter "Rideshare Provider."

Line B, Enter code from instructions. I'd suggest using 485990, Other Transit & Ground Passenger Transportation. I personally think it's more appropriate than 485300, Taxi & Limousine Service, which some sources suggest.

Line C, Business name. Unless you've incorporated your rideshare business, just leave this blank. Do *NOT* enter Uber, Lyft, or whatever company you provide rideshare for.

Line D, Employer ID number (EIN). If you applied for an EIN for your business, enter it here. Otherwise, just leave this field blank.

Line E, Business address. Simply enter your home address.

Do not enter all of the amounts you need to enter on Schedule C as multiples of $100. Unless it's actually true, which is unlikely. You'd be absolutely amazed at how many taxpayers will pull this on this form, in particular – entering both income and expense lines solely in multiples of $100. They're clearly estimating amounts rather than working from actual records (if any records exist), and they're just asking for an audit.

If you provide services for more than one rideshare company, don't prepare a separate Schedule C for each one. One Schedule C is fine for all of your rideshare income and expenses.

However, if you and your spouse both provided rideshare services, you'll each need to file a Schedule C, and an associated Schedule SE for each of you if you both showed net profits for the year.

TIPS FOR PREPARING YOUR SCHEDULE SE

Schedule SE is the document you'll use to compute self-employment tax on your self-employment income.

You'll need to prepare and file a Schedule SE, Self-Employment Tax, when the amount on line 4 of the Short Schedule SE, or line 4c of the Long Schedule SE, is $400 or more. That's the IRS' terminology. Translation: If your net self-employment income is $433.14 or more, you need to complete Schedule SE. This amount generates the "net earnings" of $400 that the schedule and its instructions refer to.

If you and your spouse both provided rideshare services, you'll each need to complete a Schedule C. If both of you showed a net profit for the year, you'll each need to prepare a Schedule SE, as well. Most software programs will generate these forms automatically, based on the self-employment numbers that you've entered..

Do not file more than one Schedule SE for yourself, and not more than one for your spouse. This could slow down the processing of your return.

If you fail to file a Schedule SE and don't pay self-employment taxes when your Schedule C shows net self-employment income of $433 or more, you should expect correspondence from the IRS after you file your return.

RELEVANT CREDITS

The Difference between Deductions and Credits

A tax credit gives you a *dollar-for-dollar* reduction of your income tax. This means that a credit of $500 will lower your $750 income tax liability to $250. However, a credit of $500 will only lower your $250 income tax liability to zero. Please note – the credits I mention below will *not* lower your self-employment tax liability.

Deductions, meanwhile, lower your self-employment income and/or taxable income. So, a $500 *deduction* will only result in a lower tax based on a *percentage* of $500.

Qualified Plug-In Electric Drive Motor Vehicle Credit

Qualified vehicles purchased after 2009 may be eligible for a tax credit of up to $7,500. The exact amount of the credit may vary, based on the capacity of the battery that's used to power the vehicle.

You cannot claim this credit for the same vehicle that you claim a credit for on Form 8910, Alternative Motor Vehicle Credit.

Qualified Plug-in Electric Drive Motor Vehicle defined. A Qualified Plug-in Electric Drive Motor Vehicle is a new vehicle with at least four wheels. It must be propelled, to a significant extent, by an electric motor that draws electricity from a battery with a capacity of at least four kilowatt hours, and is capable of being recharged from an external source of electricity. It must have a gross vehicle weight of less than 14,000 pounds.

What vehicles qualify. Generally, you can rely on the manufacturer's or distributor's certification to the IRS that a specific make, model, and model year vehicle qualifies for the credit and, if applicable, the amount of the credit that it qualifies for. However, check the IRS' website just to make sure; the IRS may have published an announcement that contradicts what the manufacturer or distributor is representing to you. Search "Qualified Vehicles Acquired after 12-31-2009" on irs.gov to see an up-to-date listing.

Amount of tax credit.

There is a maximum credit of $7,500 per vehicle. (Don't be misled by line 10 of Form 8936, the form where the credit is claimed – the maximum credit amount displayed on that line relates to vehicles with less than four wheels). There are a few things to bear in mind about the $7,500 amount, however.

First, you'll need to use your business use percentage when figuring Part II of Form 8936, where you compute the credit. But… you can also claim credit on the personal use portion of the expense on Part III of the Form.

Second … this is a *non-refundable* credit. This means that it can only offset the tax shown on line 47 of Form 1040 – and it will *not* offset your self-employment tax. So, if your tax on line 47 of Form 1040 is $3,200, you can only claim a maximum of $3,200 (or less, if you've claimed other credits on line 48 through 53 of Form 1040).

And finally, there's no carryover for this credit. That means that if you can't claim the whole amount that you're potentially eligible for in the tax year of purchase – generally because the credit has reduced your income tax liability to zero – then you can't claim the remainder of the credit in a later year.

Credit phase-out. It's also worth noting that this credit begins to phase out for a manufacturer's vehicles when at least 200,000 qualifying vehicles have been sold for use in the United States. Be sure to research before buying a particular model to make sure that the car you're interested in is still eligible for the credit. Search "IRC 30D – Plug-In Electric Drive Motor Vehicle Credit Quarterly Sales" on irs.gov for the latest data.

Where to claim the credit.

The credit is claimed on Form 8936, "Qualified Plug-In Electric Drive Motor Vehicle Credit (Including Qualified Two-Wheeled Plug-in Electric Vehicles)." The business-use portion of the credit is also reported on Form 3800, "Business Credits," and finally, carried over to Form 1040, line 54.

Please be aware that Form 8936 can be confusing when you're preparing it. In particular, the filer is directed to take different actions when claiming a credit for two-wheeled vehicles and four-or-more-wheeled vehicles. And, don't be misled where you see the "Maximum credit per vehicle" on line 10 listed as $2,500 – this applies to vehicles with less than four wheels.

Form 3800 is no great joy, either. Just try to follow the instructions as best you can.

Effect on basis for depreciation purposes. Since you're claiming business use of this vehicle, you'll have to reduce the basis of the vehicle by the amounts on line 11 and 18 of Form 8936 for depreciation purposes. This is only relevant when you use Actual Car Expenses.

Alternative Motor Vehicle Credit

Qualified fuel cell vehicles may be eligible for a tax credit, as well, but not if you've claimed a credit for the same vehicle on Form 8936, "Qualified Plug-In Electric Drive Motor Vehicle Credit (Including Qualified Two-Wheeled Plug-in Electric Vehicles)."

Qualified Fuel Cell Vehicle defined. In the IRS' words, "This is a new vehicle propelled by power derived from one or more cells that convert chemical energy directly into electricity by combining oxygen with hydrogen fuel, and that meets certain additional requirements."

What vehicles qualify. Previous versions of the Instructions for the form this credit is claimed on contained a list of eligible vehicles. Unfortunately, as of this writing, this list is not on the form or in its Instructions, nor does the IRS appear to have an updated webpage at irs.gov that lists qualifying vehicles. As with a Qualified Plug-in Electric Drive Motor Vehicle, however, you generally can rely on the manufacturer's or distributor's certification to the IRS that a specific make, model, and model year vehicle qualifies for the credit and, if applicable, the amount of the credit that it qualifies for. If the IRS publishes an announcement that the certification for any specific make, model, and model year vehicle has been withdrawn, you cannot rely on the certification for such a vehicle purchased after the date of publication of the withdrawal announcement.

Amount of tax credit.

For vehicles that weigh 8,500 pounds or less, the base credit is $4,000; an additional $1,000 to $4,000 credit may be available depending on the extent to which the fuel economy of the vehicle exceeds what's defined as the 2002 base fuel economy as enumerated in the Internal Revenue Code.

You'll need to use your vehicle's business use percentage when figuring Part II of Form 8910, "Alternative Motor Vehicle Credit," where you compute the credit. But you can also claim credit on the personal use portion in Part III of the form.

As with the Qualified Plug-In Electric Drive Motor Vehicle Credit, this is a *non-refundable* credit. It can only offset the tax shown on line 47 of Form 1040, and it will not offset your self-employment tax. So, if your tax on line 47 of Form 1040 is $2,300, you can only claim a maximum of $2,300 (and less, if you've claimed other credits on line 48 through 53 of Form 1040).

And, there's no carryover for this credit. If you can't claim the entire amount that you're potentially eligible for in the tax year of purchase – generally because the credit has reduced your income tax to zero – then you can't claim the remainder of the credit in a later year.

Credit phase-out. As with the Qualified Plug-In Electric Drive Motor Vehicle Credit, there's a phase-out for this credit, as well. As of this writing, the credit was available through tax year 2016.

Where to claim the credit.

The credit is claimed on Form 8910, "Alternative Motor Vehicle Credit." The credit is also reported on Form 3800, "Business Credits," when the car is used at least partially for business purposes, and, finally, carried over to Form 1040, line 54.

Retirement Savings Contributions Credit

This credit isn't specifically related to the rideshare business, but I hope that you're able to spend a few minutes looking at this section. It could potentially help you with your retirement. That's a long way in your future, most likely, but it never hurts to think about it. The years can roll by pretty quickly, to which I can attest.

Many people are aware of the Earned Income Credit (EIC) and Child Tax Credit (CTC), both of which apply to families with children. According to IRS Publication 4801, Individual Income Tax Returns Line Item Estimates for 2014, more than 28 million taxpayers claimed EIC, and well over 20 million took the CTC.

By comparison, fewer than 8 million taxpayers claimed the Retirement Savings Contributions Credit, aka Saver's Credit, in that same tax year. I suppose that lower number is based on a smaller level of awareness. The IRS routinely launches publicity campaigns for EIC and CTC, but disseminates relatively little information on the Saver's Credit. That may be due to the intent of each piece of legislation. EIC and CTC were designed to lift families out of poverty, in the present. The Saver's Credit was implemented to help people with their futures. If more people knew about this credit prior to tax time, they might be more inclined to take advantage of it. Hopefully this portion of the book will nudge a few folks in that direction.

(And, let me point this out, before you say, "Well, I didn't contribute to a retirement plan during the tax year." The beauty of this credit is that you don't have to have made a contribution *during* the tax year – you only have to make the contribution *before the due date of your tax return*, including extensions. The due date for 2016 tax returns is April 18th, 2017. Please read on.)

What we're looking at here is the government partially, but potentially generously, subsidizing your retirement fund, if you create one – up to 50% in many cases, while allowing you to also potentially reduce your Adjusted Gross Income, which can lower your tax.

In essence, it's free money – if you set up a retirement account and qualify as I describe below, the government will pay a portion of your contribution. So, let's see how this works.

109

Who can claim the credit?

You're eligible for the Saver's Credit if:

1.   You've made contributions to a traditional IRA or Roth IRA; a 401(k), SIMPLE IRA, SARSEP, 403(b), 501(c)(18) or governmental 457(b) plan; and/or voluntary after-tax employee contributions to a qualified retirement and 403(b) plan. (My example below refers to an IRA, but applies to any of these funds.);

2.   You are at least 18 years old;

3.   You're not a full-time student – that is, you're not enrolled as a full-time student at a school, and you didn't take a full-time, on-farm training course given by a school or a state, county, or local government agency. (There are a few more restrictions – go to irs.gov and query "the instructions for Form 8880, Credit for Qualified Retirement Savings Contributions, for the definition of a full-time student);

4.   You're not claimed as a dependent on another person's return;

5.   You file and complete Form 8880, Credit for Qualified Retirement Savings Contributions;

6.   You owe tax on your taxable income; and,

7.   Your Adjusted Gross Income (AGI) falls below certain threshold levels, based on your filing status. No credit is allowed for the 2016 tax year if your filing status is

Married Filing Jointly	Head of Household	Single, married filing separately, or qualifying widow(er)
and your AGI is more than $62,000.	and your AGI is more than $46,500.	and your AGI is more than $31,000.

Your Adjusted Gross Income for tax year 2016 will be calculated on line 37 of Form 1040, line 21 of Form 1040A.

110

It's clear that the greatest benefit of this credit will be for taxpayers with lower incomes, and I should note that the credit will only offset any tax on your taxable income. If you have zero taxable income (i.e., your AGI minus your standard deduction and exemptions is zero or negative), your credit will be zero. Likewise, if your AGI is higher than the limit shown above, read no further. However, if it is within this range, let's look at how this works.

Amount of the Credit

The amount of the credit that you're allowed is 50%, 20% or 10% of your IRA or retirement plan contributions, up to $4,000 if you're married filing jointly, and $2,000 if you're filing under any other filing status. Here's the breakdown of available credit rates for the 2016 tax year:

Credit Rate	Married Filing Jointly	Head of Household	Single, married filing separately, or qualifying widow(er)
50% of your contribution	AGI not more than $37,000	AGI not more than $27,750	AGI not more than $18,500
20% of your contribution	AGI from $37,001 – $40,000	AGI from $27,751 – $30,000	AGI from $18,501 – $20,000
10% of your contribution	AGI from $40,001 – $62,000	AGI from $30,001 – $46,500	AGI from $20,001 – $31,000
No Credit Allowed	AGI more than $62,000	AGI more than $46,500	AGI more than $31,000

If your retirement contribution is via IRA, this credit represents one of the few tax situations in which you're legally allowed to "double-dip" – that is, use the same transaction for more than one beneficial purpose. Take a look at this scenario to see what I mean.

Example. Let's say that you're married, filing your return jointly, and are claiming no dependents. Your spouse is a full-time student and not working. You're a part-time student and a rideshare partner, and earned $36,000 providing that service. To simplify things for purposes of illustration, I'll assume that this was the only income you or your spouse received during the year, and so your AGI was also $36,000. You contributed $2,400 to an IRA in 2016 (*or*, as noted earlier, before the 2016 tax return deadline of April 18, 2017.)

If you look at Form 1040 or 1040A for tax year 2016, you'll see that your standard deduction for married filing jointly is $12,600. The exemption amount is $4,050, so between you and your spouse, that's $8,100.

Without an IRA deduction, your taxable income would've been $15,300 – that's your $36,000 AGI minus your $12,600 standard deduction, and the $8,100 you're allowed for exemptions. Per the tax table, which can be found in the instructions for Forms 1040 and 1040A, the amount of tax on $15,300 is $1,533.

But, *with your IRA deduction?* Your tax drops to $1,293. In this scenario, since you've contributed $2,400 to an IRA, your AGI isn't $36,000 anymore, but $33,600. You take your IRA deduction on line 32 of Form 1040, or line 17 of Form 1040A. (A self-employed SEP deduction, SIMPLE deduction, or qualified plans deduction would be taken on line 28 of Form 1040; these can't be deducted on Form 1040A. This is technical info, I admit, but worth pointing out.) And, deducting the same amounts for your standard deduction and exemptions as above, that now drops your taxable income down to $12,900 which, again per the tax table, yields $1,293 in tax.

(**Note:** IRA deductions are generally limited to $5,500 per contributing taxpayer, $6,500 if age 50 or older but under age 70 ½ at the end of the tax year; there are also phaseouts for higher income taxpayers. Deductions for other types of contributions that the Saver's Credit can apply to can be substantially higher – see IRS Publication 560, Retirement Plans for Small Business (SEP, SIMPLE, and Qualified Plans). Sorry, this is more tech stuff, but I'm striving for as much completeness as possible in a minimum number of words.)

So, from this simple maneuver alone – deducting the amount of your IRA contribution from AGI – you've reduced your tentative tax liability by $240. Think about that for a moment – your IRA investment has just provided you a tax break of 10% of its worth. It's only a one-time benefit, but I think most people would be happy with an immediate 10% payoff on an investment.

Okay, so the reduction in tentative tax is substantial, but here comes the double-dipping part. Since you've made a $2,400 contribution to your IRA, and your AGI is $29,600 – see the chart above – your Form 8880 credit against tax is $1,000 – which offsets most of your $1,293 in tax.

So why isn't your Saver's Credit $1,200, which is 50% of $2,400? Remember – the credit can only be applied to up to $2,000 of contributions made by any one taxpayer.

Let's do a little more math here. You contributed $2,400 to an IRA. This contribution has resulted in a $240 reduction in your tax, and a $1,000 credit against the remaining tax. That's $1,240 of direct cash benefit you've received on your $2,400 contribution – over 50%. Big picture, you own a $2,400 IRA account that has cost you only $1,160, net out-of-pocket. Opportunities like this don't come along very often. That's why I'm pushing this credit.

Of course, this example is a case in which the numbers line up to get fairly close to the maximum benefit, but take a little time to toy with the numbers yourself, and see if this is a good idea for you.

And remember – I can't stress this enough – you can make this contribution up to the day before the due date of the return, including extensions.

If you're filing near the deadline

If you're like many people, you're getting your return together right before the April deadline. (Unfortunately, I've been a member of this group more often than I'd like to admit.) You've got other things to do, and don't really have time to research institutions that offer IRAs. Are there any shortcuts?

Well, yes, there is one. You'll notice that I said you have to have contributed to an IRA prior to the due date of your tax return, *including extensions*. So, if you haven't contributed by April 18th, 2017, you can file an extension, and before the extended return is due, set up your IRA account.

You do this by filing Form 4868, Application for Automatic Extension of Time To File U.S. Individual Income Tax Return, *on or before* the original April filing deadline. Be careful here, though – filing an extension does *not* allow you an extension of time to pay your taxes.

That's right, you still have to pay your taxes by the filing deadline. So, you'll need to prepare a "dummy" Form 1040 of your return with all of your income items, the IRA deduction and the Retirement Savings Contributions Credit, and any other items you'd have on a return if you were to file it timely. And, if the return shows a balance due, you need to enter your total tax liability amount on line 4 of Form 4868, and remit that amount with the 4868 by the April due date of the return. (Do *not* file your "dummy" Form 1040 with this! You'll cause both the IRS and yourself countless problems.) This allows you an additional six months to shop around for an IRA vessel that fits your needs, and then file your return. If the dummy return shows a refund, you don't need to send any money with the extension.

MANAGING YOUR RIDESHARE BUSINESS

While it may be too late for you to do these things in time for this tax season, here are some thoughts about what you should do in preparation for the next one.

Make Estimated Tax Payments as needed

For the moment, at least, rideshare drivers are considered to be contractors, and therefore no taxes are withheld from the payments you receive from the service. The burden is on you as a self-employed person to not only withhold these taxes, but submit them periodically to the IRS.

(Please note that this book is focused on federal income tax, but let me also point out that, if you live in a jurisdiction with state income tax, you may need to submit estimated tax payments to that state's authority, as well.)

The American income tax system is based on a pay-as-you-go model, which means that you must pay income tax (and generally, Social Security and Medicare tax, as well) *as you earn or receive your income* during the year.

When you earn wages as an employee, this payment is taken from your wages by your employer and sent directly to Uncle Sam. But when you're self-employed, this burden falls entirely upon you.

As a wage earner, you provide your employer with a Form W-4, Employee's Withholding Allowance Certificate, so that the employer can withhold the correct amount of federal income tax from your pay. The amount withheld from each of your paychecks is based primarily on your level of income and the number of exemptions you anticipate claiming on your federal income tax return.

And your employer also withholds Social Security and Medicare taxes. This isn't based on your W-4; rather, it's calculated on what your projected annual income would be, based on each pay period. These are the amounts you see in boxes 4 and 6 of Form W-2, Wage and Tax Statement, which the employer is required to provide you before tax season.

When you're in business for yourself, you're responsible for withholding all of this – not only income tax withholding, but Social Security and Medicare withholding, as well. And since the tax system is pay-as-you-go, you generally need to make estimated tax payments.

This is some serious business. The IRS requires that you make these payments *every quarter*.

What if you haven't made these payments, or underpaid? If you've underpaid your estimated tax throughout the year – even if you pay the amount in full when you file your taxes – you may be assessed a penalty for the underpayments of estimated tax during the tax year.

It's possible that you won't owe estimated tax payments for any given quarter, but it's best to run the numbers and see, rather than face a penalty. Use IRS Form 1040-ES, Estimated Tax for Individuals, to estimate your tax and determine if a payment is due. If so, submit this form to the IRS along with your quarterly payment. See also IRS Publication 505, Tax Withholding and Estimated Tax, available at irs.gov, for more information.

There are also apps and websites available that can automatically calculate your estimated taxes, taking your current and projected income and expenses into account.

So what constitutes an underpayment as far as the penalty applying? You may owe a penalty for 2016 if the total of your withholding and your timely-made estimated tax payments didn't equal at least *the smaller of either* 90% of your 2016 tax, or 100% of your 2015 tax. Mull that over for a bit.

The underpayment tax penalty is paid by filing Form 2210, Underpayment of Estimated Tax by Individuals, Estates, and Trusts, with your tax return. Most income tax software will automatically calculate the penalty, and generate Form 2210 for inclusion with your tax submission package.

If you don't file this form with your return or figure the underpayment, the IRS will figure the penalty automatically and send you a bill once the return is processed. For more information on the underpayment penalty, see Form 2210 and its instructions.

If you should have a refund coming to you when you file your tax return, you might consider applying it toward next year's taxes, if you know you're going to have to make an estimated tax payment, anyway.

116

You can do this by entering the desired amount on line 77 of Form 1040, "Amount of line 75 you want applied to your 2017 estimated tax." This amount must be less than or equal to the amount on line 75, which reflects the amount of taxes you overpaid.

If you compute the overpayment on line 75 of Form 1040 correctly, but don't reduce that amount by the combined amount of your estimated tax election (line 77) and any estimated tax penalty (line 79), your return will fall out during processing and be looked at by a Tax Examiner. The examiner will adjust your entry on line 76a, "Amount of line 75 you want refunded to you," by subtracting the sum of the estimated tax election and estimated tax penalty from the overpayment.

If the refund line (line 76a) and your estimated tax election line (line 77) have identical amounts and you didn't claim estimated tax payments on line 65, the examiner will delete your estimated tax election from the record – that is, you'll receive your refund, and the estimated tax payment you requested on line 77 will not be applied to next year's tax.

If the refund line (line 76a) and your estimated tax election line (line 77) have identical amounts and you *did* claim estimated tax payments on line 65, the examiner will delete your refund. You won't receive a refund, but the amount will be applied toward next year's tax.

Set up Business Accounts

Technically, you're allowed to use a personal account if you're a sole proprietor. You can have rideshare earnings deposited into your personal account, pay for related business expenses out of that same account, and take your "draw" from the account.

In the real world, though, this is just a terrible idea.

Co-mingling your business and personal funds is asking for trouble. Seriously. Over time, you're liable to forget which expenses were personal and which were business, and come tax time, you might undercut or overstate your business expenses.

From an IRS standpoint, it's a recipe for disaster. In the event that you're audited, you'll be required to provide statements and receipts showing the business use of business expenses. If you've conducted your business via your personal accounts, this will probably require the auditor to sift through your records. There are four good reasons you don't want this to happen.

First, if certain items don't seem to be business-related *on their face,* the auditor will most likely disallow their associated deductions. You will *probably* have the opportunity to provide more information, depending where you are in the audit process, but you need to understand that the burden is on you – the taxpayer – to "prove up" your deductions. If you're records aren't sufficient, this is a basis for disallowance.

Secondly, you want to make the audit as painless as possible for the auditor. It's clear that audits are very stressful for the taxpayer. But please consider, your auditor probably has cases piling up in her cue. Do you really want her wasting a lot of time on your audit case? Keeping your auditor happy with what you've provided could result in a more favorable result for you. Technically, it shouldn't matter, but in reality it does.

Thirdly, if your self-employment in the rideshare service somehow results is a loss for the year, the co-mingling of funds will likely persuade your auditor that you're running your business as a hobby. In loss situations, the IRS has to make a very basic decision as to whether you're carrying on a business or a hobby. (Rideshare driving wouldn't seem like simply a hobby to most of us, but that's not important here.) One of the primary factors the IRS looks at in determining whether you're participating in a business or a hobby is whether you've carried on your activities in a business-like way. The lack of a separate business account suggests a hobby. But, you may ask – why does it matter whether this service is a hobby or not. Quite simply, if your activity is determined to be only a hobby, your loss won't be allowed. That is, your business expenses will be limited to the amount of income for that business.

And, number four of the reasons to not comingle your business and personal accounts: you *really* don't want an auditor looking through your personal expenses when you're being audited for your small-business activities. You don't have to use much imagination to guess what might happen if the auditor comes across large purchases for extravagant items, even if they're clearly for personal use. Although the scope of your audit might have originally just been business deductions... audits can be expanded. And even if this doesn't happen,

118

the auditor's opinion can be colored – the reasonableness of your personal expenditures could potentially influence how she perceives the reasonableness of your business expenditures.

So… make it easy on yourself, and on a potential auditor. Open up a separate account for your rideshare business. (And if you should have another non-rideshare small business, open an account for that one, too.) It'll not only save you headaches in keeping your business records separate, but it will also make it much easier to gauge how well your small business is actually doing.

When you need money from your business account for personal expenses, simply write yourself a check or electronically transfer it to your personal account, being sure to note that this money was for personal rather than business use.

One warning, though – and this may seem logical, but you'd be amazed at how many small business owners do this – *do not* deduct amounts as business expenses on your tax return when that money was for personal use! For more information, see my essay on "Draw" in the Deductions portion of this book.

My personal experience with credit unions has been wonderful, and many of them allow sub-accounts within your personal account for no additional fee. A drawback, though, is that you might not be able to have a credit or debit card associated with that sub-account.

When you open up a dedicated business bank account, there are likely to be fees related to both the account and any associated credit or debit card. It's my view that these are well worth it, in view of the clear separation you create from your personal accounts. And, is you'll also see in the Deductions section, these fees are deductible from your business income.

Keep Good, Up-to Date Books

As with keeping separate financial accounts, the main reason to keep up-to-date records is organization. It's much easier to remember the details of transactions while they're fresh on your mind than to struggle reconstructing them later.

There are a lot of apps out there that can help minimize the pain of recording all of your transactions. Some of these are offered for free, but bear in mind that if you pay for them, they'll be deductible form your business income, to the extent that they're used for the business.

A very good – and *free* – resource is IRS Publication 583, Starting a Business and Keeping Records. This Pub provides basic federal tax information for people starting a business and gives sound advice on recordkeeping.

Consider an Employer Identification Number

An employer identification number, or EIN, is a nine-digit number similar to a Social Security Number (SSN) that the IRS assigns to businesses. You most likely don't need one – it doesn't seem probable that you'll have employees, which is really the main reason for an EIN.

However, there are other good reasons to apply for one.

If you want to create a self-employed retirement plan, you'll probably need an EIN.

Using an EIN – as opposed to your Social Security Number – for business purposes can shield your SSN from overuse. Your SSN is much more attractive to a potential fraudster than an EIN. You always want to keep your SSN as private as possible, and using an EIN for business activities will cut down on your Social Security Number's use and visibility.

Finally, using an EIN as opposed to an SSN can also demonstrate that you're serious about keeping your business activities separate from your personal activities, an important issue for IRS audit purposes that I described earlier in the book.

Apps, apps, apps!

Along the same line, there are a number of apps out there that help you track activities important to rideshare – primarily, receipts and mileage. If there are costs involved with the apps, they're deductible to the extent that they're used for your business.

APPENDICES

Appendix 1 – Section 179 Deduction Limitations

Limit on the amount of the Section 179 Deduction

For 2015 the total amount you can elect to deduct under Section 179 generally cannot be more than $500,000.

If the cost of your Section 179 property placed in service in 2015 is over $2,000,000, you must reduce the $500,000 dollar limit (but not below zero) by the amount of cost over $2,000,000. If the cost of your Section 179 property placed in service during 2015 is $2,500,000 or more, you cannot take a Section 179 Deduction.

The total amount you can deduct under Section 179 each year after you apply the limits listed above cannot be more than the taxable income from the active conduct of any trade or business during the year.

If you are married and file a joint return, you and your spouse are regarded as one taxpayer in determining any reduction to the dollar limit, regardless of which of you purchased the property or placed it in service.

If you and your spouse file separate returns, you are regarded as one taxpayer for the dollar limit. You must allocate the dollar limit (after any reduction) between you.

For more information on the above Section 179 Deduction limits, see Publication 946.

Limit for sport utility and certain other vehicles

For sport utility and certain other vehicles placed in service in 2015, the portion of the vehicle's cost taken into account in figuring your Section 179 Deduction is limited to $25,000. This rule applies to any four-wheeled vehicle primarily designed or used to carry passengers over public streets, roads, or highways, that is not subject to any of the passenger automobile limits explained under Depreciation Limits , later, and that is rated at no more than 14,000 pounds gross vehicle weight. However, the $25,000 limit does not apply to any vehicle:

121

- Designed to have a seating capacity of more than nine persons behind the driver's seat,

- Equipped with a cargo area of at least 6 feet in interior length that is an open area or is designed for use as an open area but is enclosed by a cap and is not readily accessible directly from the passenger compartment, or

- That has an integral enclosure, fully enclosing the driver compartment and load carrying device, does not have seating rearward of the driver's seat, and has no body section protruding more than 30 inches ahead of the leading edge of the windshield.

Limit on total Section 179 Deduction, special depreciation allowance, and depreciation deduction

Generally, the total amount of Section 179 Deduction, special depreciation allowance, and depreciation deduction you can claim for a car that is qualified property and that you placed in service in 2015 is $11,160. The limit is reduced if your business use of the car is less than 100%. See Depreciation Limits, later, for more information.

Appendix 2 – Election not to claim the special depreciation allowance

On a separate page attached to your tax return, include the following, with your relevant information:

Your Name, or the name of your company

Your Social Security Number SSS-SS-SSSS (or Employer Identification Number, NN-NNNNNNN)

Tax Period Ending December 31, 2016

Election to Not Claim Special 50% Depreciation Allowance

Per Internal Revenue Code Section 168(k)(7), taxpayer hereby elects not to claim the special depreciation allowance for the following asset classes placed in service during the tax year ending 12/31/2016:

Five-year property [to elect out of only the class applicable to passenger vehicles]

All eligible classes of property (to elect out for all property)

Appendix 3 – Maximum Depreciation Deduction for Cars

Date Placed

In Service	1st Year	2nd Year	3rd Year	4th & Later Years
2012 – 2016	$11,160*	$5,100	$3,050	$1,875
2010 – 2011	$11,060**	$4,900	$2,950	$1,775

*$3,160 if the car was not qualified property or if you elected not to claim the special depreciation allowance.

**$3,060 if the car was not qualified property or if you elected not to claim the special depreciation allowance.

For previous year deductions, please see IRS Publication 463, Travel, Entertainment, Gift, and Car Expenses

Appendix 4 – Maximum Depreciation Deduction for Trucks and Vans

Date Placed

In Service	1st Year	2nd Year	3rd Year	4th & Later Years
2016	$11,560*	$5,700	$3,350	$2,075
2015	$11,460*	$5,600	$3,350	$1,975
2014	$11,460*	$5,500	$3,350	$1,975
2013	$11,360*	$5,400	$3,250	$1,975
2012	$11,360*	$5,300	$3,150	$1,875
2011	$11,260*	$5,200	$3,150	$1,875
2010	$11,160*	$5,100	$3,050	$1,875

*If the special depreciation allowance does not apply or you make the election not to claim the special depreciation allowance, the first-year limit is $3,560 for 2016, $3,460 for 2015, $3,460 for 2014, $3,360 for 2013, and 2012, $3,260 for 2011 and $3,160 for 2010.

For previous year deductions, please see IRS Publication 463, Travel, Entertainment, Gift, and Car Expenses

REFERENCE MATERIALS

2016 Instructions for Schedule C
Form 8910, Alternative Motor Vehicle Credit
Form 8936, Qualified Plug-in Electric Drive Motor Vehicle Credit
Instructions for Form 1040
Instructions for Form 8910, Alternative Motor Vehicle Credit
Instructions for Form 8936, Qualified Plug-in Electric Drive Motor Vehicle Credit
Internal Revenue Manual
Publication 334, Tax Guide for Small Business
Publication 463, Travel, Entertainment, Gift, and Car Expenses
Publication 529, Miscellaneous Deductions
Publication 535, Business Expenses
Publication 544, Sales and Other Dispositions of Assets
Publication 560, Retirement Plans for Small Business (SEP, SIMPLE, and Qualified Plans)
Publication 583, Starting a Business and Keeping Records
Publication 946, How To Depreciate Property
Publication 4801, Statistics of Income – 2014 Individual Income Tax Returns Line Item Estimates
Schedule C (Form 1040), Profit or Loss From Business
IR-2015-137, 2016 Standard Mileage Rates for Business, Medical and Moving Announced

ABOUT THE AUTHOR

John C. White is a licensed attorney, and he worked for the Internal Revenue Service for more than twenty years as a Tax Examiner, Revenue Officer and Tax Analyst.

As a Revenue Officer, he was the Technical Assistance Coordinator and Self-Employment Tax Coordinator for the Austin, Texas, Examination, Underreporter and Accounting functions. In these capacities, he provided detailed tax law opinions on thousands of complex individual income tax issues over the course of several years.

As a Tax Analyst for almost a decade, he wrote software requirements for the IRS' Modernized eFile and Error Resolution Systems. In 2016, he received the prestigious Commissioner's Award for his work writing the requirements necessary for implementation of the Affordable Care Act.

John received a Bachelor of Journalism degree from the University of Texas in 1985, and a Juris Doctorate from the University of Arkansas in 1988.

He lives in Fayetteville, Arkansas with his wife, Melissa.

Made in the USA
Coppell, TX
07 April 2022

76184302R00075